Angels Bloom

A mother's story of struggles and fight for life of a newborn child

Kim C. Thai

Angels Bloom

ISBN: 978-1-945975-19-6

Published by EA Books Publishing a division of

Living Parables of Central Florida, Inc. a 501c3

EABooksPublishing.com

Angels Bloom

DEDICATION

✝

In Loving Memory of

Valerie

September 22, 2014
January 8, 2015

∞

"The Lord's Prayer"

Our Father who art in heaven,

Hallowed be thy name;

Thy kingdom come;

Thy will be done on earth as it is in heaven.

Give us this day our daily bread;

And forgive us our trespasses

as we forgive those who trespass against us;

And lead us not into temptation,

but deliver us from evil.

Amen

ACKNOWLEDGMENTS

I would like to thank all the doctors, nurses, and caretakers who provided care for Valerie while she was alive, and my family and friends who supported me during this difficult time. Especially, I would like to thank my friend Justina and her sister Teresa for the development and design of the Angels Bloom Foundation website. In particular, I would like to acknowledge the support from my daughter and husband. I would also like to acknowledge my coworkers for their sympathy and understanding. Finally, a special thank you to Father Patrick at our beloved Catholic church in Virginia.

Angels Bloom

CONTENTS

FOREWORD

Angels Bloom is an unusual work in that it weds concrete medical and detail-focused information with a very personal spiritual journey. Rarely are two such disparate subjects brought together and woven so thoroughly to develop such an emotionally—and intellectually—compelling case.

It can be difficult to find meaning in the hardest parts of life, to pinpoint the silver lining or the lesson to be learned. But we take something from every challenge we face, and at best we learn a productive, useful lesson, rather than absorb a lesson or attitude that will not serve us well.

Kim Thai is certainly the right person to author this particular book, given her medical background, knowledge, and expertise—as well as her analytic skills and curious skepticism about spiritual matters. Had she been too easily convinced of her message, too ready to accept the views of her husband and in-laws, she might have made a less persuasive argument.

She takes us through a complex series of events, giving us a full picture of the challenges that she faced through her daughter Valerie's illness and the supports that helped so much. Because she describes her husband's attitudes toward spirituality, we gain the opportunity to see more than one perspective on the issues at hand.

Kim's quest for understanding both centers on and eases her daughter's medical challenges. Facing a daughter with a rare cardiovascular disease is terrifying both because of the enormity of the potential consequences and because of the tremendous responsibilities that come along with parenting in such a situation.

She juggles Valerie's needs along with those of her older daughter, Olivia, as well as those of her husband and extended family. Because Kim is so strong, even more is asked of her. She even handles extensive home repairs—which, by themselves have been known to faze many a strong person—in the midst of Valerie's fight for her life.

Probably the biggest challenge, though, is the search for meaning in everything that is happening. Kim's husband points to communication from Angels and messages from beyond that bring comfort and meaning to their lives. But Kim brings to bear her extensive scientific and analytic background and questions whether life can truly be preordained. With her intense research and analytic abilities, she is determined to try to control the situation, a situation that simply cannot be controlled. Kim is a fighter, and realizing that acceptance can be a useful tool, in fact a vital fact of life, is a challenge for her.

It is not until Valerie passes, then returns—in a manner of speaking—to convey messages to her mother and to the rest of her family that Kim learns the importance of hope and the relevance of

Angels, of advice from beyond.

As we see Kim yearn and develop through her experiences, we grow along with her. She does not even realize she's on a spiritual journey. She thinks she's just trying to take care of her daughter and the rest of her family, trying to tend to her own needs and desires, and she hungers after meaning. It is that openness toward finding meaning that enables Kim to achieve a new level of spiritual understanding.

This spiritual understanding has brought Kim to devote her life to bringing hope, love, and compassion to children with rare congenital diseases and their families. This book shares Kim's journey to find meaning. And in seeking meaning, she learns to listen to the Angels who are trying to help us make sense of our lives. These Angels, Kim learns, exist both in this world and beyond. And they reach out to us, to share messages about our own lives, messages that help us better understand what is happening. With this knowledge, we can—it is hoped—learn to accept the harder parts.

Kim brings us this spiritual message in the hope that it can help us—in the face of tremendous medical and personal challenges, and sometimes even without being tested so rigorously—to face life with more strength, dignity, and love. Kim is teaching us to learn to accept love when it comes, accept knowledge as it arrives, and bring it into our lives in a way that encourages love and life and meaning.

By joining her intellectual rigor, meticulousness, and integrity with her heart open to messages that, perhaps, come from outside medical and academic circles, Kim shows us a new path. And she invites us to join her on it.

PREFACE

This book was written in response to the life and death of Valerie, my second of three daughters. She was with us for three months, sixteen days, and six hours, but she died following a surgical procedure that attempted to treat her rare heart condition.

My hope is that this book, by recounting the story of one child with a serious congenital illness and the journey I went through as her mother, will provide support to the families of other children with similar illnesses and, at the same time provide inspiration and hope for the children themselves.

Valerie has inspired us to start the Angels Bloom Foundation, Inc. in her memory as well. Another purpose of this book is to support the foundation, to provide the resources we need to help others.

Angels Bloom Foundation is a tax-exempt organization under section 501(c) 3 of the U.S. tax code. It is dedicated to bringing hope, love, and compassion for children with rare congenital diseases. Our mission is to offer support, education, and hope to families affected by rare congenital diseases, through support groups and public awareness. We focus on bringing hope to families, with the idea that "Where Angels Bloom, There is Hope."

Our major goals include being a leading support group center for families who have children with these desperate illnesses, providing resources to help these families find other support group help, as well as assisting them in gaining additional benefits—emotional, physical, and financial—for their children.

We also hope to let families know that they are not alone and to provide emotional support for the caregivers as well as the patients. For instance, it is normal for a mother to feel that she is not doing enough, even though from an outside point of view she has done everything she possibly could to assist her child. We want to let mothers, fathers, and other family members and friends know that they are admired, appreciated, and loved for the courage they have shown to live through this.

The foundation works with individual donors, charitable foundations, and corporations to help care for children with rare congenital diseases. It funds its services and activities largely through selling books and through donation support.

More information on the Angels Bloom Foundation can be found at our website, www.angelsbloomfoundation.org.

It is what Valerie would have wanted.

INTRODUCTION

This is a book about my journey to find meaning, my journey to gain understanding and to learn to listen to the Angels who are trying to help us make sense of our lives. The Angels, both in this world and beyond, attempt to give us messages about our lives so that we can better understand what is happening and accept the harder parts.

It can be difficult to appreciate our place in the universe, to realize that while we can manage some aspects of our lives, there are others that are simply beyond us, beyond our ability to control.

My experiences with my daughter Valerie taught me this lesson. And I am sharing my story in the hope that other people can learn from my journey so that they do not have to gain this understanding the hard way as I did. Here is my story.

At twelve weeks into my pregnancy with my second daughter, Valerie, I had my first ultrasound. The routine imaging test showed that the fetus had only a two-vessel umbilical cord, instead of a three-vessel umbilical cord that most babies have at this point.

The umbilical cord is sort of a supply line to the growing baby. Most babies have three vessels within the cord: one to bring oxygen and nutrients into the body and two to get rid of the waste, through the mother's body. In about 1 to 2 percent of cases, there are only two vessels—like with my baby. Doctors do not know what causes this condition, which is also called two-vessel cord. This condition has been known to be associated with a variety of birth defects, including problems with the heart, central nervous system, and urinary tract, as well as chromosomal abnormalities.

My husband and I were worried about this situation, as we knew that the development of the heart and brain take place at the same time, and we were afraid that the two-vessel umbilical cord might not carry enough blood to Valerie to allow for full and normal growth of these vital organs. We also knew that, while the majority of babies with a two-vessel umbilical cord are born without any major birth defects, there are a small number of babies that do have some issues that relate to the heart and sometimes to the brain as well. In addition, I had a miscarriage at eleven weeks with my second pregnancy. My physician had not heard a heartbeat at that point in the pregnancy so sent me to get an ultrasound. This diagnostic test showed that the fetus had stopped developing at around six to eight weeks. For this reason, I was particularly nervous about my pregnancy with Valerie.

Due to potential problems associated with the umbilical cord, our doctors kept an especially close watch on my pregnancy from that point onward. Around my twentieth week of pregnancy, about halfway through, I had another ultrasound and Valerie was diagnosed with hypoplastic left heart syndrome (HLHS).

In HLHS, the left side of the heart has not developed properly and is thus too small to properly carry out its primary function, which is pumping oxygen-rich blood routed to it from the lungs to the rest of the body. HLHS is a rarely occurring birth defect. The standard treatment for this condition is a series of multiple surgeries, typically a set of three surgeries called the Norwood, Glenn, and Fontan, respectively. Usually, infants receive the Norwood operation immediately at birth, the Glenn (or Hemi-Fontan) procedure when they are three to six months old, and the Fontan surgery somewhere between eighteen months and five years of age. Of course, these surgical procedures vary from person to person.

However, for smaller and/or premature babies, surgeons may suggest what is called a hybrid procedure before the Norwood procedure. A hybrid procedure typically involves both surgery and cardiac catheterization (insertion of small plastic tubes into the patient's veins and arteries to diagnose or treat conditions). Valerie underwent intensive treatment, including a successful hybrid procedure, but, despite this, she died at the age of three and a half months. She had not yet had the Glenn or the Fontan procedure.

But that was not all we learned. In addition to the HLHS finding, the twenty-week ultrasound also showed a cystic structure in the inferior portion of the brain, which is the lower part of the brain stem. A cyst is a tiny bubble of fluid that has been pinched off and is similar to a blister. Such cysts may not be harmful in and of themselves, but there is some evidence that they may occur somewhat more often in fetuses that have abnormalities in their chromosomes. Generally, cysts go away long before the baby is born. Of course, all this is speculation and nothing can be confirmed until after the baby is born or with a more invasive procedure.

We were given the option to abort the baby at that time, but we decided not to. We did not even move forward with any invasive procedures like an amniocentesis, which might have given us more information about Valerie's health problems, but carried a small chance of causing a miscarriage. It is a medical test that involves taking amniotic fluid from inside the placenta. This test is usually done so that the DNA in cells from the fetus, which are normally found in the fluid, can be checked for various genetic issues or concerns. Although there was only a slight possibility of miscarriage from the amnio procedure, we did not want to take that risk, especially given our experiences with my previous pregnancy.

We were determined that I would carry her to full term and give her a chance of life. Since we were going to keep the baby no matter what the test found, it seemed pointless to endanger the baby's life for no good reason. So, instead, we waited for the next four months worrying and feeling helpless, until she was born.

At the time Valerie was diagnosed, my husband was working in a private practice with his father and brother as a family physician and I was working as a clinical project manager in cancer research. We had a healthy three-year-old daughter, Olivia, and lived in a suburb in Northern Virginia. All of my husband's relatives lived nearby and all of my relatives lived in New Jersey where I had grown up. My husband is the second eldest out of four boys, three doctors and a dentist. I am the youngest of a family of five boys and five girls. We had a strong support system, which was very important as we struggled through Valerie's many medical challenges.

Both of our families are first-generation immigrants from Vietnam. Fortunately, language was not an issue for us; that can sometimes be a real problem when dealing with the health care system. Support from family is very important for my husband and me.

Our religious beliefs were also very important in helping us through everything that happened. Faith, I have found, is critical. Although I had grown up in a Buddhist family with many superstitious beliefs, I believe in one God and one family, so I converted to Catholicism before my marriage. My husband and I have similar religious beliefs.

Valerie's diagnosis was the start of a journey for which I did not feel prepared. Up to that point, I had had almost no experience with serious illnesses, nor did I have to bear that responsibility either, the responsibility of having to care for a particularly sick person. However since, my husband is a physician, he certainly has experience with illness and with death. But he had never personally dealt with a severe illness and death of a close family member, specifically that of his own daughter. It is one thing to deal with a patient's death and watch the family experience that pain; it is completely different when it is your own daughter, your own family.

Similarly, my experience with death had been very limited prior to Valerie's birth. My cousin Hong died about five years previously from cancer. I was fortunate not to have known anyone personally who had died before her. She was only forty-two years old at the time and left three daughters (then ages six, ten, and fifteen) and her husband behind. The husband is still a single father, raising three children on his own. Knowing she was leaving behind her children must have been incredibly difficult for my cousin.

Hong's funeral was the first and only funeral I had ever attended in my life. It was surely a dramatic experience for me. It is not easy for anyone to go to a funeral, and the first one is always an eye-opening experience. Her funeral upset me for weeks afterwards. It was something I had a hard time dealing with; losing a loved one is hard enough without having to go to a funeral as well.

The immediate aftermath of Hong's funeral was even more

meant to bring hope to all the children out there who were born with an illness that left them with very little hope and very little chance of survival.

The friends and family who know our story have told me that I did everything humanly possible for Valerie. But as a mother, I do not really feel that way. I always question myself and think that I could have done more to possibly change things. Many people have approached me and commended me for the effort that I made. To me, it was not enough. I am no more spectacular than the next mother.

It is a mother's instinct to protect her child and I do not feel that there is anything spectacular about what I have done. It was my job as parent. But subconsciously, I know that that is not true either. Even if I knew I had to do what I did, that does not mean it was easy. And I think it is important to celebrate all the efforts I—and other mothers—put into taking care of our fragile children.

I want to tell other mothers out there that they are spectacular. Not every mom out there is willing to give her entire life up to care for a child. The amount of stress that mothers experience during that time, and possibly for the rest of their lives, is truly enormous. Perhaps it is also an inner struggle during the grieving period of shock, denial, pain, guilt, anger, bargaining, depression, acceptance, and hope.

I know I did a lot for my baby, but I always question whether if I had found a different hospital, with surgeons who had more experience dealing with HLHS, it might have been different. Valerie's situation was something that had to be fixed with surgery, rather than treated medically, and part of me believes that the outcome might have been different had we found different health care providers. I will also, in this book, share some of my encounters with Angels and how they have helped me through this difficult time. I believe in Angels in general, both in this world and beyond, and I believe Valerie is an Angel, as she has shown us many signs. Angels are very real and if you can bring your Angel into your life, then it will be easier to accept and handle the many challenges that life throws at you. Because, alas, those challenges are inevitable. And it is through meeting them that you learn how strong you really are.

Chapter One

THE END RESULT MAY NOT BE THE SAME

Without hope there is no chance of survival, no chance to set concrete goals and to use the enormous power inherent in optimism and faith. This is something you hear often, tagged on many motivational posters. But it is not just something to say—it is real. It is true. Without hope you have nothing, and no shot at survival. I learned this myself the hard way, something I wish on no one. I wish I had known about the link between hope and survival when Valerie was first diagnosed with her condition.

My husband's family kept saying, "The end result may be the same." It was a frustrating thing to continually have to hear. They were convinced that we only needed to enjoy our limited time with Valerie, rather than focus on helping her to survive. But I was concentrating my time and energy on trying to improve and lengthen Valerie's life, believing strongly in the power of positive thinking to make change manifest.

I would ask them, "Well, what is the end result? Would someone please tell me?" For the longest time I could not understand why they said the things they did. I found it all just so confusing. Was I the only one that believed that things could be different? Now I know that they just did not believe in Valerie's survival. I needed to believe that she would survive but things were different for them. As much as they wanted to have hope, it was difficult for them to believe in that miracle.

But I could believe in nothing else. I wanted, needed, for Valerie to survive.

My father-in-law, brother-in-law, and husband are doctors; therefore, it was difficult for them to have hope for Valerie. They were looking at things from a scientific and medical perspective, whereas that was the last thing that I wanted to hear. I wanted to know that there was still a chance that my daughter would live through this ordeal. I had hope for Valerie because I loved her so much and perhaps was in complete denial of the situation. As her mother, I did not leave myself a choice to think otherwise. I had to be her biggest advocate, because she surely could not fight on her own. If I did not have hope, then I would not have the strength to fight alongside her. And I just could not bear letting her go. It was not a choice. It was love and a mother's natural instinct for her child.

Again, I am writing this book to encourage the mothers, fathers, and those who have loved ones suffering from incurable illnesses to have hope. Not necessarily hope of long life, but at least hope that the loved ones will enjoy their last days and experience at least a little bit of the precious joy of human life. Above all, it is so important to have hope in all aspects of your life. Hope is the reason for our existence and it also enables us to bring a dream into reality.

Children harness hope at an early age and have no problem with hoping for all sorts of things throughout their young lives. We tend to lose hope and become pessimistic as we get older and learn more about life. This is especially true for those from a scientific background, where everything needs to be logical and proven. These people need facts and diagnoses. Holding out for hope is not part of their worldview or of their life plan.

After the death of Valerie, I now believe that not everything in life must be logical or make sense. Her death in itself never made sense to me. And most importantly, I believe that with hope, "the end result may NOT be the same." I appreciate what my husband was trying to tell me. But I think understanding something intellectually is not the same as knowing it in your heart; through her life and through her death, Valerie taught me this lesson in its most essential form. Believing in something and having hope is essential to getting through the hard times that everyone has at some point in their lives.

I now believe in Angels and that we all need to have Angels in our life. I believe that we all have a Guardian Angel whom we can call upon to help us in times of difficulties. In fact, there are many Angels around, but at least one of them is devoted especially to each and every person.

While I believe that our destiny is predetermined, that everything is written and will happen as predicted, I also believe in the importance of being good and kind to ourselves and to others. There are some things that we can change—not necessarily how many children we have and how many will reach adulthood—but certainly we can control the quality of life that they enjoy.

One way that we can do that, that we can extract every bit of love and joy possible from our lives, is to listen to our Angels. They will tell us what is inevitable and what we can modify or alter. By focusing on what is possible, we can make sure that our efforts have the greatest possible impact. Rather than spinning our wheels on, say, trying to get Valerie to live longer than she was predestined to live, I could have been concentrating on making her final days as pleasant and loving as possible. I believe that is what my husband's family was trying to tell me.

The doctors told me that Valerie would not make it, and my husband's family sent the same message. And I could easily have gotten the same information from my Guardian Angels, if I had listened to them. And if I had, it would probably have been easier for both Valerie and myself.

Valerie was a gift from the Angels. She was a gift for the time that we had her; she was never meant to stay. But she was a powerful force for good and for love while she was here.

This story is, in part, about my learning to listen to Angels, to realize that we can accept our fate and at the same time improve the quality of our lives.

I did not believe in Angels until after Valerie died. Her final days would have been more peaceful had I realized that she was an Angel, that there are so many Angels around and active in our lives.

Valerie is my Angel and she will always be in my heart. I know she is up there in heaven watching over me. She plays with my eldest daughter Olivia, watches us throughout the day, and sleeps with us at night. I can feel her there with me at all times. Her spirit surrounds me, giving me the strength and encouragement to move on with life, to have hope for others, including my husband, our marriage, our day-to-day life, and our newly expected baby girl. Valerie has forever enriched my life, my husband's life, and the lives of everyone she touched—family, friends, and even the people in the hospital who had the chance to see her beautiful face and personality.

I hope that this book will show other people the lessons that I learned and help them to appreciate Angels without having to go through the experiences I did with Valerie. I would like the challenges I experienced to benefit others. That would represent yet one more gift Valerie gave to the world.

Chapter Two

VALERIE-HANA

Due to health problems associated with the two-vessel umbilical cord and the cyst in Valerie's brain, I was referred to the office of an obstetrician/gynecologist who specialized in high-risk situations. I remember lying on the examination table there for three hours, cold and scared, wondering about the results of the ultrasound. A few minutes can feel like an eternity when you are waiting for important news. You sit and worry and wait while wondering if you are about to hear the worst news of your life. It is hard on the heart as well as the spirit. You hope for so much and it never makes the waiting any easier. That's the hardest part, waiting to find out if your prayers have been answered.

After careful review of the ultrasound, the high-risk gynecologist came and told me that my baby had hypoplastic left heart syndrome. He explained to me what that is, but my mind was

7

not listening. I was in shock, hungry at that point, and my body was shaking. As I was crying, I told him that my husband is a doctor as well and asked if he could call my husband directly to explain.

After being told about the baby's heart condition and many hours researching on the condition, my husband and I still decided that we would keep her. We named her after Saint Valerie for being valiant, strong, and courageous because we knew she would need that strength to survive. We wanted to name her Valerie-Hana, which can also mean strong family. I always love the name "Hana" from the Road to Hana in Maui, which means the "road to heaven." We went to Maui on our honeymoon and I found it to be one of the most beautiful roads that I had ever seen. However, after hearing from family and friends about the superstition of children with heavenly names and how it correlates to illnesses, we decided to drop the Hana. (I heard this both from Buddhist relatives and from one of the doctors, a Catholic with a Mexican background, who told me that most of his heart patients have names like "Nevaeh," which is the reverse of "Heaven.") Valerie was still such a beautiful name that we were more than happy with our choice.

We chose to not move forward with an amniocentesis. We wanted our sweet Valerie no matter what, regardless of what the future held for our little family. You never know what could happen, and to decide about something while Valerie was still in the womb just did not make any sense to me. This was especially true in Valerie's case. We knew she would be undergoing a surgical procedure, and possibly more than one, after her birth. So we wanted her to be born as big and healthy as possible, to give her the best possible chance to survive and thrive.

As a Catholic, I believe that life begins at the time of conception, so we did not want to abort the baby. We never even considered the possibility of terminating the pregnancy, so it did not matter to us whether there were genetic issues with the fetus. No matter what we might learn from the procedure, we would not act on that information, so we decided not to take the chance, however slight it might be. As Catholics, we believe that you take what God gives you, and we knew he would give us exactly the Valerie that we needed in our lives.

Week after week, I prayed for a miracle, that somehow the diagnosis was false and that the heart was not as underdeveloped as the echocardiogram showed. Mistakes could be made—you never knew. I just wanted her little heart to be okay. This level of hope was extremely difficult to maintain, as my husband and I work in medicine and science. The biological reality is much closer to us than it is to other people. That reality is something that you just cannot deny, but still we remained hopeful.

During this time, I had a dream that my baby died. In my dream, as in real life, I saw my husband and myself waiting in the hospital while the doctors were operating on Valerie, trying valiantly to save her life. After a bit, we spoke with the doctor, who apologized for not being able to save Valerie. We saw her lying on the bed, black and blue. It was a very upsetting dream.

Looking back on it, I could have seen this as a message from the Angels, but at this point, I just took it to mean that this was my worst nightmare. I still wanted to do everything I possibly could to keep my baby here, on earth, with us all.

Since my baby was very small, there was a high risk of miscarriage. I went on bed rest for the remainder of the pregnancy. I kept hearing from the doctors that the baby was not going to live. During this time, I had ultrasounds every two or three weeks and became very depressed. My husband and I took a trip to the National Shrine Grotto of Our Lady of Lourdes in Emmitsburg, Maryland, to pray and bring back holy water. I bathed, soaked myself, and drank the holy water. What else could we do, other than pray for that miracle? While the tests indicated that she had an imperfect heart, we could still hope that the tests were wrong, that Valerie had a beautiful four-chambered heart. We could hope and pray that the medical situation was not as worrisome as we had been led to believe.

I tried to get second and third opinions about Valerie's prenatal diagnosis. I spent endless hours on the Internet researching HLHS and the top children's hospitals, heart centers, and surgeons. I reached out to the Boston Children's Hospital, the Children's Hospital in Philadelphia, and even as far away as the Texas Children's Hospital, where my husband's cousin, Trung, is a pediatric intensivist. I spoke extensively with Trung and could tell that while he was trying to be optimistic, he had a sense of what the end result would be. Trung gave me very helpful advice, such as the need to keep daily logs of Valerie's condition, noting any improvements or changes. I thought about taking Valerie down to Texas so Trung could examine her but decided that the travel was too risky. But when Trung came up to visit us over Christmas, he examined Valerie and reassured me that we were doing the best we could for her.

There are only two hundred babies a year born with hypoplastic left heart syndrome in the United States, so the number of programs with the expertise to treat this condition is rather small. I read up on the three best children's programs, which were in Boston, Philadelphia, and Houston.

I contacted the Children's Hospital of Philadelphia (CHOP) first because that was the closest hospital to my parents' house in New Jersey and we knew a few people there. In particular, I reached out to Dr. R., a cardiologist and medical director of the Fetal Heart Program at CHOP. This program specializes in the detection, evaluation, and management of fetal heart defects prior to a baby's birth and offers a team of leading experts in the diagnosis of fetal heart defects such as HLHS. It offers a multidisciplinary team of experts and the most advanced imaging technology available and is the largest and most experienced comprehensive fetal heart program in the world.

Unfortunately, because we live in Virginia with two children's hospitals nearby, the insurance considered CHOP to be out of network and coverage was denied. Although the hospital in Virginia was not well known for treating children with heart problems of Valerie's type, it did have a doctor with appropriate expertise.

Dr. R. at CHOP wrote two appeals to our insurance company, which I thought was extremely kind of him—more than I would have expected. But, unfortunately, his appeals fell on deaf ears and did not help get us coverage to have the procedure performed at CHOP. I took that as a sign from the Angels and accepted that there had to be a reason for the denial. Perhaps Valerie's path was already laid out and it was God's way of letting her stay closer to home with me, Olivia, and her father.

In any case, the practical issues of going to the hospital in Philadelphia would have been immense. Because I was on bed rest and thus multiple long trips were not appropriate, because I had to undergo frequent tests, and because I could, in theory, go into labor at any time, I would have had to move to Philadelphia. Since my husband could not leave his job for that long, I would have had to go either alone or with Olivia. I had no relatives in Philadelphia, but my husband's family was here, in the greater Northern Virginia area.

While I understood that it made no sense to uproot the family and move to Philadelphia for who knows how long, I was angry that we did not do so. I was annoyed both with myself and with my husband. While the Angels were starting to make sense to me, I still was not prepared to fully believe in them and their message.

I pushed hard to get the doctors and health care providers to move things along, but when that did not work, I became very discouraged and angry. I was not sure what to do. Then I took a step back and prayed, which helped me to be able to just let life unfold. I began to hear voices inside me, which guided me day to day.

I kept thinking that if we could get Valerie through this stage—through this day, week, month—she would be fine. Everything would be okay. The constant ups and downs were very hard on me. Finally I realized that I had to accept that there were certain things I could not control. It's very difficult to think about that, especially with something as treasured as a little baby. But I had no choice.

In the meantime, we tried to prepare for the birth in other ways. We were living in a two-bedroom condominium in a high-rise, which we thought would be too small once we had another child. We also wanted to live closer to Fairfax Hospital, since we were anticipating that Valerie would need frequent treatment there over an extended period of time. Nevertheless, I thought it might be best to put the move off for a while. My husband, however, wanted to go ahead with it. I think the move and the work on the house gave him something other than Valerie's health issues to think about.

In any case, we found and bought a house near the hospital, but unfortunately, we made a bad choice. The house required extensive work. In fact, it had to be gutted. We hired a contractor to do the work, but unfortunately the contractor left the job halfway through the project. My husband had to quickly find help and essentially became the general contractor himself. We had to hire various contractors to finish up the work. I was on bed rest while making phone calls all day to obtain quotes for the unfinished work. My brothers from New Jersey drove down to help with the house every weekend. Our goal was to have the house in livable condition before September, which was my due date. We worked until September, and my brothers and sisters came from New Jersey to help us move, unpack, and buy furniture. Buying the house was certainly a distraction for my husband, as he had intended. Unfortunately, it added a lot of stress, both mentally and financially, as the renovations cost more than twice the amount we budgeted.

Chapter Three

TWO VIVID DREAMS WHILE PREGNANT

After knowing of Valerie's heart condition, I had two vivid dreams. The first was at twenty-five weeks gestation. I was in a deep sleep, when I felt the presence of Hong, my cousin who had passed away about five years previously. I knew that there was a reason why she was in my dream. I never saw her face, but I knew it was she.

I asked her that if something happened to my baby and she did not live, she would take care of her in heaven. It was so important to me to know that there would be someone to look after my daughter if she passed, as I would no longer be able to. The thought broke my heart but I had to ask her anyway. My cousin Hong agreed and replied that she would be there to care for Valerie when she passed. But she had a request of her own that I was more than happy to oblige. In return, I must give her three daughters some money to help them. I quickly agreed; how could I not? Dreams are weird and yet while you are in them they make perfect sense. I actually never saw her face or talked to her in the dream, but somehow understood that it was her and the agreement we made.

Another vivid dream I had, which became a reality, was with Valerie. I hoped dreaming about Valerie would always be a good experience. I saw myself in the hospital, outside the operating room waiting. Waiting for what, I was not sure. Waiting for news? For Valerie to come out? Was I waiting for good news or the kind of news I hoped I would never have to hear about? Like I said before, waiting was often an experience that made time stand still or at least slow to a crawl. Sitting there waiting, I felt scared and helpless. The doctor came out and told me to come in to see Valerie, as they could not save her. I could not imagine hearing worse news than that. That's the moment when time really does stand still. Not only that but you have to ask yourself if you even hear the news correctly. Did they really say that they could not save my Valerie? What exactly did that mean for me, for her? At that time, I thought it was just a bad dream. It had to be, right? Little did I know that the Angels were preparing me to accept what was about to happen.

At this point, I did not think much of the dream. It just was not meaningful then. But now, as I look back on it, it was very meaningful.

After Valerie passed, my cousin Hong's daughter Van told her father that she had a dream and that her mother was taking care of a little baby. Van said that her mother claimed that the baby belonged to auntie.

Van did not know who Valerie was or what had happened to her. This was definitely a message from the Angels and Van was just a conduit. The dream did not mean anything to her—but it meant a lot to me.

Since then, I have been extremely loyal to Hong and her family. I give them financial gifts every three or four months, at every holiday and then just periodically. After Van's dream, I have made a commitment to help out Hong's husband and his three daughters as much as I can, for the rest of my life. I am sure that dream was a message from the Angels and I also believe that the Angels were telling me to look out for Hong's family.

Chapter Four

THE POWER OF HOPE

After knowing Valerie's heart condition, I had monthly checkups with the pediatric cardiologist for echocardiograms. An echocardiogram is a way of examining a heart by means of ultrasound waves. The waves are sent through the patient's body by means of a wand, and the heart reflects the waves back. Images of the heart are constructed from those reflected sound waves.

When an echocardiogram is performed directly on a patient, the technician presses the wand directly against the patient's skin and moves it over the patient's chest. When the patient has not yet been born, the technician instead presses the wand against the mother's skin and moves it across her abdomen.

The echocardiograms were not conclusive. All tests done before delivery, when the baby is not yet born, are speculative.

Testing can identify a condition, but the severity is unknown. Hope is still there. After birth, however, the ultrasound test can confirm the degree of severity. Nevertheless, it was clear well before birth that Valerie had heart problems, even if we could not yet be sure of the details or of the degree of severity.

Dr. E., the pediatric cardiologist, somehow always knew how to cheer me up and provide hope for the situation, which I was most grateful for. I was a big believer in hope and he knew this. His compassion for the situation helped give me the encouragement I needed to carry on. That was the most important thing after all, finding a way to carry on no matter what.

Dr. E. was also great at explaining Valerie's condition to me. He would draw his own pictures of the heart, and he explained what HLHS is in simple terms geared for lay people, until I told him that my husband and I are in the medical and scientific field.

Chapter Five

DELIVERING VALERIE

Valerie had extreme intrauterine growth retardation. This condition is an abnormally slow growth of a fetus. When the baby is born, it appears small for its actual age. Intrauterine growth retardation is associated with an increased risk of illness and death in the newborn period.

The doctors did not think she would make it past thirty weeks of pregnancy. Imagine knowing that your child may not be in the womb that long. It is just a lot to take in and more than a lot to have to live with. But I was determined to help her stay inside as long as possible, in order to grow more, to come out as healthy as possible, and to have a fighting chance at life. We wanted to give her the best possible chance of surviving the surgical procedure that we knew was all but inevitable.

The doctors had encouraged me to deliver Valerie more than three weeks early, but we refused to, as my husband and I thought that it would give her a better chance with the heart surgeries if she was bigger in size. We hoped for a big and healthy baby to help her as much as possible. We had a long road ahead of us, and making sure Valerie stayed in the safety of my womb for as long as possible was a big deal to us. So we took the chance of me carrying her longer, so that she could grow, despite the doctor's warning that that might stress the baby and cause a miscarriage. That was the last thing that I wanted, but I felt that carrying her as long as possible was the right thing to do.

My little fighter stayed in there longer than they had expected, and I was proud of her fighting spirit. The doctors again were concerned that Valerie might not be strong enough to withstand labor and a natural birth, so they encouraged a scheduled C-section. In fact, Valerie did better than was expected, my girl made the whole trip. She made it to full term, and at 40 weeks, on September 22, 2014, I brought my beautiful daughter into this world through a scheduled cesarean section in the hospital.

The C-section was scheduled at 4:00 p.m. but was delayed by almost an hour due to an emergency within the hospital that the other doctors had to attend to. My husband stood by me waiting for the baby to come. It was the moment we had been waiting for the whole nine months. We were about to meet our new daughter and greet her not only into our life but also into the world around us.

She was special and I could not wait to hold her.

For the C-section, I was given epidural anesthesia and my lower abdomen was screened from my view, so, although I was awake and alert, I could not see or feel the surgery while it was in progress. The C-section was quick and over before I knew it. All of a sudden I heard a cry. They scooped her up, cleaned her up, and brought her to me. I cannot even begin to tell you what it felt like to have her with me finally, snuggled in the crook of my arm. She was the most indescribably sweet, beautiful creature I had ever seen. Any child of mine would be precious—but given Valerie's fragility, her tenuous hold on life, it seemed particularly important that she know how treasured, how cherished, she was. My Angel sitting there in my arms as if she belonged nowhere else. This was what she was meant to do, where she was meant to be.

No words can quite describe the feeling. Unless you have children of your own you will never know the sheer immediate love that comes when you bring life into the world and lay your eyes on her for the first time. It was a miracle; every birth is a miracle and Valerie was no exception. I could have held her like that for hours. But alas, I could not do that, as there was work to be done on Valerie's little heart.

My husband took a picture of Valerie with his phone so that we would have something to gaze at. He knew in his heart that we would not have Valerie for long and he wanted to treasure every moment, revel in the short time we had to spend with her. I continued to hang onto my optimism that something would happen, that Valerie would live a long life. But my husband read the signs from the Angels and anticipated that her fate was not to stay with us for long. We both wanted to appreciate every moment we had with our baby girl.

The doctors stabilized Valerie and then rushed her to the neonatal intensive care unit (NICU), so that she could receive the care she needed for her congenital heart disease as well as for her small size. (Her birth weight was only 1,820 grams, or 4 pounds, and she was 44.5 cm, or 17 inches long.) I wish I could say she came right back but I did not see her for the next two days.

Unfortunately, I developed a fever and could not see Valerie again immediately. Postoperative fever is relatively common in the first few days after surgery but it might have been caused by bacterial or viral infection, so I was given antibiotics prophylactically. The NICU has very sick babies, so it does not want anyone to enter who might be contagious. That includes anyone on antibiotics, until they have taken the antibiotics for at least two or three days.

The NICU only allowed the baby's guardian/parents and two other designated relatives to visit. So only my husband and his parents were able to see Valerie. My husband took pictures so that I could see Valerie, but that just made me more anxious.

From my point of view, the wait might as well have been forever. I longed to see my baby, to hold her once again. I understood that she needed to be cared for in a way that I could not provide quite yet. The doctors finally cleared me of the infection and let me into the NICU to see Valerie. It was the best news of my life.

When I saw Valerie for the first time in the NICU, it was a shock. She was attached to wires and monitors and needed oxygen. I was afraid to pick her up and hold her, as there were just too many wires. Her heart was highly unstable, and unlike us receiving 100 percent oxygen, she was only receiving about 70 percent to 80 percent oxygen. The good news is that she was able to breathe on her on and was not intubated. This means that she did not need a machine to help with her breathing.

Valerie was in NICU Room 200. I looked around the room and most of the babies were just as unstable as Valerie. They were mostly premature babies that could not breathe on their own, with multiple developmental issues. Each nurse was assigned to two to three babies in their twelve-hour shift. Room 200 was an open area with about six to ten babies. The neonatologist would make rounds between the other NICU rooms of about one hundred beds throughout the day.

During the first two weeks in the NICU, Valerie was fully examined and multiple tests were performed, including genetic testing. She was monitored by cardiology, who performed an echocardiogram, which showed a complex congenital heart disease. Although hypoplastic left heart syndrome was the worst of all her cardiac problems, she had others, including sinusoids (small and irregular vessels linking coronary arteries which supply oxygen-rich blood to the entire heart muscle), septal heart defects (openings in the walls between the different chambers of the heart), and a defective heart valve. There was, however, also some modest good news; the arachnoids brain cyst seen in the echocardiograms during the pregnancy had disappeared before Valerie was born. Nevertheless, although we were not fully aware of it at the time, this was the beginning of her journey to fight for her life. It was going to be a hard road and we needed to prepare to help Valerie fight.

Holly, the geneticist coordinator, called us in for a family meeting with the neonatologist, cardiologist, geneticist, social worker, and nurse to discuss Valerie's case. My husband and I came to the meeting not knowing what to expect. The geneticist, Dr. S., informed us that Valerie had Wolf-Hirschhorn syndrome (WHS). Dr. S. explained to us that Wolf-Hirschhorn syndrome is the result of a genetic abnormality, in which chromosome 4 does not contain all the genetic information that it should. This causes a number of problems, including mental retardation and abnormalities of several organ systems, including, in Valerie's case, the heart. The syndrome is known to cause multiple organ failures and defects, which may progress later on in life. Children with WHS are very slow to develop basic motor skills. The syndrome also affects their appearance. They are typically short and have a particular type of facial features. Even if Valerie overcame her heart repair, she would still be faced with an untreatable illness and some serious disabilities.

The neonatologist, Dr. W., asked us if we wanted to consider DNR (do not resuscitate). My husband and I, in a state of shock, simply agreed. Dr. W. told us to think about it and let her know the next day. She somehow knew that we would change our mind about the DNR, which we did the next day. My husband and I tried to stay strong and asked questions about the syndrome. As a physician, my husband already knew that the odds were all against her. Being born with HLHS is devastating, and now the added factor of a genetic syndrome made any chance of long-term survival more complicated. It certainly was not looking good, but I was determined to hold out hope for her and a for miracle to come. Dr. E. gave me a hug and reminded me what I told him before I delivered Valerie. I said that Valerie was a gift from heaven, and I would be grateful for however long she stayed with us. Meanwhile, I would enjoy whatever time we had with her.

My husband and I drove separately, so he walked with me to the front of the hospital. He took off and I waited for the valet to get my car.

I sat on the bench and broke down in tears. I felt a hand on my shoulder and looked over. The valet grabbed me and gave me the tightest hug ever. There was a glow on her face and over her head, like a halo. She asked me if I was okay and I mumbled to her that my baby was going to die. She told me that if that happened then "it is because this life is too hard for the baby. And God does not want the baby to suffer. But be assured that he will bring you another one and that baby will be perfect." I felt her words of wisdom soak through my skin. It helped me stand up from that bench and gave me the strength to get through the deepest sorrow that day. I normally do not listen when I am upset, but I felt her words sink into my heart and I really believed in them. There I was, getting comfort and support from a complete stranger, as if the Angels had sent her to help me. With those few words, I found hope and strength to accept the situation. Nevertheless, there were times when things got worse for Valerie and I did not trust those words. I now know and believe that it was a message from the Angels to help me through that time.

I went home that evening and researched Wolf-Hirschhorn syndrome. I saw pictures of children with the syndrome and felt helpless. I had never heard of such an illness before. Something I did not even know about a week earlier was now having an enormous effect on my life.

A million thoughts flew through my mind. I wondered: What does it feel like to be a child living with this syndrome? If it were me, would I want to continue to live with this syndrome? Would it bother me to be so different than everyone else, to not fit into what society defines as normal? Not only how would I feel but, more important, how would Valerie feel? I cried all evening but by morning I somehow realized that it is not for me to choose how or whether Valerie wanted to live. I recognized that I had to accept what God had chosen for Valerie and just help her as much as I could and to give her love and comfort.

Chapter Six

TIME IN THE NICU

Valerie was in the NICU for about a month. I was out on maternity/medical leave, so I was the full-time mom taking care of her. My husband, as a doctor, had to work all day, so was only able to visit Valerie at night. My mother came from New Jersey to help cook and watch Olivia for the first few weeks after Valerie was born. My doctors advised me not to drive for the first two weeks following my C-section, but five days after I had been released from the hospital, I had no other way to go to see Valerie, so I drove anyway. It was very tiring and very painful. It was a lot to juggle at the time, but I wanted to keep a normal schedule for Olivia as well. I would take Olivia to daycare in the morning and stay with Valerie in the hospital until I had to go pick Olivia up. After my husband got home from work and his visit at the hospital, I would go back into the hospital most nights until midnight to check up on Valerie again.

There were some very attentive nurses in the NICU who took very good care of Valerie. I am forever grateful for the love, compassion, and sympathy they had given Valerie during her stay. Meredith was one of the nurses whom I felt Valerie really loved, and hence stayed calm with. She went out of her way to find Valerie a more comfortable crib. Meredith decorated the crib to look more like a home crib, rather than a hospital bed. She would visit Valerie, even when she was not assigned to work in Room 200. Meredith worked and celebrated her birthday with Valerie. With tears in her eyes, she held Valerie and told her the she would "crawl out of this hospital." I too could not hold back my tears.

The NICU had its own way of doing things. They called both babies and parents by their last names, so, Valerie was called "Thai Baby" and I was called "Thai Mom" instead of our real names.

Valerie was not alone in her brief journey through life. During her stay at the NICU, there was another baby there with very dedicated parents. "Juan Baby," too, was very ill and prayer was needed. He was born prematurely and not all his organs were sufficiently developed.

I talked to some of the other mothers in the hospital and most of them told me that their husbands did not know how to handle the situation and told their wives to take care of everything.

The one exception was the Juan family. "Juan Mom" was there every time I was there; she became one of the familiar faces I saw at the hospital. She sat praying for "Juan Baby" all day long (or at least it certainly seemed that way) until "Juan Dad" got off of work and stopped by to visit. They were certainly a strong team together, working as hard as they could for their little one. They had a schedule. Once "Juan Dad" arrived, they would pray together, then go eat in the hospital cafeteria, and then come back and sit with the baby until nine or ten o'clock at night, when it was time to go home.

The love, hope, and compassion I saw for that baby was overwhelming, which in turn encouraged me to be strong. The Juan family was a true inspiration to anyone going through a struggle in life. I knew that I had to stay strong just like they were, because Valerie needed it. And watching the Juan parents helped me to see how it was done, how to give my daughter the love and support she needed in her desperate fight.

There was also a flip side to this. As mothers often do, I never felt like I was doing enough for my baby. The Juans were such dedicated parents that I felt I had a hard time living up to them. I was doing the best that I could as a mother but it still did not feel like enough, nothing comparable to the Juan family, even though I knew intellectually that I was still doing the best I could for

Valerie. People do not understand the stress of a mother who is going through the serious illness of a small child and the tradeoffs that she needs to make.

Valerie was going through a hard time during her stay in the NICU. She faced many challenges early on. She needed to be intubated right after birth, because she needed help with breathing. Intubation involves inserting a tube through the mouth and then into the airway. The tube is connected to a ventilator, which pushes air into the lungs.

Initially, we tried to give her milk by mouth. The hospital, in fact, encouraged breastfeeding. Drinking by mouth was too much work for Valerie, however. Her heart simply could not provide her with oxygen to do even the simplest of tasks. She could not even bottle-fed, although bottle-feeding requires less work and energy from an infant than breast-feeding does.

During her second or third week in the NICU Valerie also needed to have intravenous (IV) lines inserted into her arms, so that medication and fluids could be administered through them, rather than by mouth, but the staff had trouble inserting the lines. No matter what they tried during the week they could not insert an IV line. Finally, the cardiac surgeon had to intervene, poking Valerie over forty times. She was bleeding badly and they had to intubate her again. Finally, they brought her into surgery and placed a central venous catheter (CVC), as an alternative to an IV line. Of course, there is always the risk of infection or other problems with a CVC, so the doctors suggested that her cardiac procedures take place as soon as possible, so that the CVC could be removed quickly.

Valerie underwent a percutaneous balloon atrial septostomy on October 13, 2014. In this procedure, a hole that is present between the atria of the hearts in fetuses, but that closes up in the weeks following birth, is enlarged to keep it open. This is accomplished by inserting a catheter or thin tube into the patient's veins and using it to guide a balloon to the heart and to insert it into the hole between the atria. Once in place, the balloon is inflated to stretch the hole between the atria.

Valerie was then scheduled for a planned hybrid procedure ten days later, on October 23, 2014. In the meantime, the hospital put Valerie on hormones called prostaglandins to maintain the cardiac system that allows for reoxygenation and circulation of the blood before birth, even though the lungs are not yet working. This system consists of an extra blood vessel, the ductus arteriosus, which creates a pattern of blood flow that is functional for the fetus, but which generally closes itself after the first breath is taken. If the vessel does stay open following the birth, the name changes to "patent ductus arteriosus" (PDA).

In Valerie's case, since the left side of her heart was too underdeveloped to take over the task of sending oxygenated blood throughout the body, prostaglandins was given to leave the patent ductus arteriosus open, so that it could continue to do that task. Her doctors hoped that if they kept the PDA open, they would be able to postpone her first surgery until she was bigger and thus had a better chance of surviving it. Unfortunately, the Wolf-Hirschhorn syndrome prevented Valerie from growing like a normal baby would. She gained no weight at all in the three weeks at the NICU. Her doctors took a chance and went ahead with the surgery; although they performed a hybrid procedure, rather than the Norwood procedure, the first of the standard set of three surgeries for hypoplastic left heart syndrome as originally intended, the surgery was just as risky. It is difficult to think of such a small little person having to go through such a serious operation. No child should ever have to experience such a thing.

The hybrid procedure used on Valerie took the work of the prostaglandins one step further. The surgical goals were to keep the patent ductus arteriosus open indefinitely, by inserting a stent, while decreasing the amount of blood circulating to the lungs, by putting bands around the major vessels leading to the lungs. The overall purpose of the procedure was to improve Valerie's blood circulation enough to allow the next procedures that were more invasive, more dangerous, and more complicated to be put off until Valerie was in better shape and more likely to respond well to them. Greater age and size, as well as better overall health, decrease surgical risk for babies. The hybrid procedure can also be a bridge to a heart transplant for babies who need a new heart, which we considered but getting to the top of a waiting list for a baby heart is not easy.

The hybrid procedure for babies with hypoplastic left heart syndrome draws on both surgical and cardiac catheterization processes and avoids the major drawbacks of both. Although incisions have to be made in the chest for the hybrid procedure, it is not as invasive as the Norwood procedure and does not require the heart-lung machine. For this reason, it was an appropriate procedure for Valerie, given her size.

Cardiac catheterization is a procedure to diagnose or treat heart diseases with a long thin tube called a catheter which is inserted into a vein or an artery. The doctor performing the procedure can, with the help of X-rays, guide it through the patient's veins until it reaches the heart. It is possible to perform a number of cardiac procedures by means of catheterization, but catheterization is not an appropriate approach for a small baby, at least until the baby's vessels have grown enough to accommodate the insertion of a catheter and its movement through the veins to the heart.

Because the hybrid procedure requires direct access to the heart and large vessels around the heart through the chest incision, doctors can directly insert a catheter into a large vessel near the heart, instead of relying on other veins/arteries on the surface of the body such as arms and feet. Using hybrid treatment that involves both surgery and catheterization makes certain types of treatment more widely available, especially to babies and may save the lives of babies who can tolerate this process but could not survive either open-heart surgery or traditional catheterization procedures. Due to Valerie's small size and the state of her health, a hybrid procedure was the best choice.

Nevertheless, the surgery was still a risk and we were afraid for Valerie. We wanted her to have the original sin remitted; clearly she had not had time to commit an actual sin, but we did not want her to possibly pass with the original sin on her soul. We believe that there is a strong connection between baptism and salvation and we wanted the very best for our little girl, both in this world and the next.

We wanted Father Patrick to baptize Valerie right there, in the NICU. We felt particularly close to Father Patrick because he had helped us figure out what to do with the miscarriage remains.

At that point, we had walked into the church carrying the miscarriage remains. It had been Father Patrick's first day with the ministry. We asked him what we should do. He told us that we could bury the remains with small children—but we were not comfortable with that. Eventually, we found a different priest in a different church who had a solution for us. But we really appreciated the concern and compassion that Father Patrick displayed—and his efforts to find a solution within the ministry that would be meaningful for us. We felt a strong connection to him.

It was about two o'clock in the morning the night before Valerie's major heart procedure when we called Father Patrick and asked him to come to the NICU. We also asked Valerie's godparents to come, but only her godmother, my sister-in-law, was available to come to the hospital on such short notice. But we really wanted Valerie to have the holy sacrament.

Having visitors in the NICU, even adult visitors, was against the hospital rules. We asked the nurses for special consideration, given the circumstances, and they were very kind to us.

The baptism was a short ceremony. Father Patrick recited a few blessings and sprinkled holy water on Valerie while she was in the special crib. Valerie was awake and alert throughout the entire ceremony, as though she knew something special was taking place.

For my husband, the baptism represented insurance that she was freed from the power of darkness and brought into the realm of the freedom of the children of God. He wanted to be sure that Valerie had the grace of salvation before she passed—which he thought would happen sooner rather than later. I never, ever thought anything like that, as long as Valerie was alive.

For me, though, the baptism took on a different meaning. I

was confident that prayer, Father Patrick's blessing, and the holy water would help the procedure to go smoothly and successfully. I saw the baptism as a way that we could help Valerie to survive.

The next morning was Valerie's hybrid procedure. My husband and I walked with the nurses while they took her down to the operating room. They told us that the surgery would take a few hours. My husband and I walked aimlessly around the hospital pretending to be strong. I wished for a Xanax during those hours. We visited the hospital chapel to pray. Finally, the surgeon called and said the procedure was a success and Valerie was back to her room. What a miracle.

Valerie tolerated the hybrid procedure well and continued to progress. Unfortunately, during her initial postoperative period, Valerie struggled with low oxygen levels in the blood. As a result, she still had very little energy. We had hoped that she would be able to feed by mouth after the hybrid procedure, but she still needed the nasogastric (NG) tube for feeding.

At one point Valerie's oxygen was so low, about a 60 percent saturation level, that Dr. G., the pediatric intensivist, came in and suggested we consider a do not resuscitate order. He asked if we really wanted to put her through all of this. He told us the reality of Valerie's condition, but I did not want to listen. I was furious. I thought Dr. G. should not be treating my daughter if he did not believe in her potential success. My husband supported me and the pediatric cardiologist on call that night, a mother herself, Dr. R., was in total silence.

It was eventually decided that the bands placed around the arteries to the lungs during the hybrid procedure were too tight and were reducing Valerie's oxygen supply. The original stent was also thought to be too small. She was taken back to the operating room for loosening of the right pulmonary artery band and the insertion of a new stent via a redo sternotomy on November 19, 2014.

My husband and I were very worried. The original hybrid procedure was taking enough toll on little Valerie; we were worried that a second procedure, so soon after the first, might be really hard on her tiny body. I thought again about Children's Hospital of Philadelphia and their greater experience with these types of medical issues. And I wished, one more time, that I had been able to arrange for Valerie to be treated there.

The reason Valerie needed a second procedure was that she had outgrown the stent that the surgeon had initially used. While she was not growing very quickly, the stent just was not doing the job anymore and Valerie needed a larger size.

My husband trusted me to make decisions and to keep up with everything that was going on with Valerie. Even though he was a physician and I am not, he knew that I am intelligent and a good researcher and I would keep a careful eye on everything to do with Valerie. He told me, though, that it is very important to trust your surgeon. "Once you start questioning your surgeon, you make your life a lot more difficult," he said.

Before Valerie went through the second hybrid procedure, we wanted to bring Olivia into the hospital to meet her little sister. We decided that it was time. But the NICU did not allow children below age eighteen to come onto the ward. In addition, it was flu season, which meant that there was an even greater than usual chance that Olivia might be carrying some germs that could be dangerous to Valerie and the other infants in the NICU.

My husband took Olivia to the toy store so that she could pick out some playthings to give to Valerie. We knew Valerie would not be playing with them, at least not right away, but it seemed important to give Olivia the opportunity to give a gift to her sister, a gift that would be meaningful at least to Olivia. So she picked out several items at the store.

When they got home from the store, Olivia sat down with a piece of construction paper and her favorite red crayon and drew a picture for Valerie. She covered the paper with red hearts to show her love for her little sister. My husband and I were very touched that she wanted to give so much to Valerie.

I was a little worried, though, that Olivia would be scared when she saw Valerie. When she saw me after the C-section, when I was ill and attached to various monitors, she got nervous. And now it would be Valerie hooked up to all the machines. The little baby was so tiny and had so many tubes coming out of her body, all connected to different scary-looking machines.

I spoke with a woman in the Child Life Center. Child Life is a unit in the hospital that helps families through this difficult time by making the stay as comfortable as possible through activities and so on. In addition to assisting children who are patients, they also run activities for patients' siblings in the waiting area.

The woman gave me a little baby that was covered in the same sorts of wires and bandages that Valerie was. Both I and my husband shared the doll with Olivia, explaining what all the tubes did and why they were helping to keep Valerie alive. We told her that Valerie wanted to get healthy so she could come home and play with her big sister. Olivia seemed to understand the situation and, since her father is a doctor, she seemed fairly comfortable with all the medical devices. We wanted her to feel as though it was all familiar, so she would not be shocked when she saw Valerie.

Olivia continued to feel comfortable with all of that, even when she came into the NICU to meet Valerie. She spent about an hour with her baby sister, talking and singing to her and smiling the whole time. It really seemed as though Valerie smiled back, too, even though babies that young typically do not know how to smile yet. And Valerie never smiled at all, which made me realize what the valet said was true. That is, this life was too hard for her, as she was in too much pain.

At one point, my husband asked Olivia if she was afraid, if she knew what a particular tube was for. Olivia said she was fine, then explained that the tube was for feeding Valerie. We were so relieved; we had clearly done a good job preparing Olivia and arranging that this visit would be a meaningful experience for her.

I was so thrilled to see the strong connection between the two sisters. I had always wanted to have a second child, ever since I gave birth to Olivia. Olivia seemed happy and connected to her baby sister. That felt like a huge gift to me and my husband.

After that, though, unfortunately we had to think about medical issues again; we felt like it might never end. It seemed like she spent a lot of time going back to that operating room. In fact, altogether, Valerie had several surgeries and was intubated six times. It was heartbreaking to watch her struggle through these procedures. I hated hearing about it. I just wanted it to be over with, to have her make it through and be okay. Was that really too much to ask? I just wanted my little Valerie to be safe and healthy.

Chapter Seven

TIME IN THE PICU AND AT HOME

Valerie tolerated the second procedure well, and was transferred to the pediatric intensive care unit (PICU) in a stable fashion. After the procedure, there was for the first time enough oxygen in her blood (the doctors' goal was to have her oxygen saturation rate somewhere between 75 and 85 percent), and she continued to progress well. Her sternal incision, the major incision down the center of her chest, over her breastbone or sternum, was closed using staples, because she had had problems with wound healing in the past and the use of wound VAC therapy, a special type of bandage, did not help much. This time around, there were no specific problems with the wound. She was still, however, having problems with feeding.

A speech/swallowing specialist performed an assessment and

recommended continued nasogastric feeding. In this method, doctors insert a thin plastic tube through the nostril, down the esophagus, and into the stomach. Then it is possible to deliver food and medicine directly into the stomach. It is often used for premature infants and other patients who have difficulty eating or drinking on their own. While it serves an important purpose, nasogastric feeding has some disadvantages. Insertion is difficult, the tube is uncomfortable, it can cause infection, and the baby never feels hungry. As I discuss in more detail elsewhere, it also makes feeding more difficult for the baby's caretakers. Worst of all, the baby can accidentally aspirate or inhale some of the milk and then get aspiration pneumonia. Nevertheless, the speech/swallowing specialist thought nasogastric feeding was necessary, so that Valerie would get enough calories to survive and grow.

Valerie's doctors had wanted to send her home after the initial hybrid surgery, but then her oxygen saturation levels dropped. Having insufficient oxygen in the blood can indicate difficulties with breathing and circulation. It requires careful monitoring and sometimes you have to administer oxygen to the patient. The doctors could not determine why Valerie's oxygen saturation levels were dropping and were concerned that it might indicate some illness. Because of the need for careful medical attention, the doctors decided that Valerie needed to stay in the hospital.

The nurses at the hospital had become very attached to

Valerie. She was there, in total, for a month—in addition to the month she spent in the NICU. According to the Society of Critical Care Medicine, most patients spend just a few days in an intensive care unit, so the nurses really got to know Valerie more than most children.

I spent most of the day, every day, in the PICU. I was there all day long while Olivia was at her Catholic day care. Then I would take Olivia home and when my husband returned from work, I would head back to the PICU for a few more hours with Valerie.

Sometimes, my husband went to the hospital to see Valerie and I stayed home and spent some time with Olivia. And sometimes my mother would come over and take care of Olivia so both my husband and I could spend time with Valerie. It was difficult to juggle taking care of two children living in two different places.

I spent much of the time holding Valerie. She wanted to be held like any other baby. In fact, studies have shown that when a mother holds her baby, it has a calming effect on the child. I played classical music a lot, and Valerie seemed to find it very soothing. When I could, I would sit in the rocking chair and rock her gently. But I had to be very careful because, depending on the position, sometimes the slightest movement would twist the wires and then Valerie would not get all the oxygen, medicine, or food she needed to survive and thrive.

The problem with my visiting—and holding—Valerie so often was that she became accustomed to being held and now wanted to spend all her time in my arms or the arms of one of the PICU nurses.

Valerie ate mostly breast milk, which I pumped regularly. I was glad for that, because I know that breast milk is the best possible food for an infant. But because of Valerie's medical condition, she needed to gain weight fast. So the hospital fortified the breast milk with formula into the NG tube.

Unfortunately, Valerie gained almost no weight, which worried all of us.

On Thanksgiving Day, we sneaked Olivia into the hospital again. As we had learned before, children below age eighteen are not allowed in the PICU. Carol from Child Life brought Valerie a little turkey stuffed animal and drew a turkey from Valerie's handprint.

Because of the holiday, the ward was very quiet. The nurses pretended that they did not see Olivia come in. Olivia brought Valerie a picture, which she had drawn, and we hung it by her bed. We ordered hospital food for the three of us to have a Thanksgiving lunch, and then we spent the morning and afternoon at the hospital. While we were there, one of Valerie's doctors came by to check on her and answer any questions we had.

Olivia was happy to see Valerie again and wanted to hold her. We were not sure if that was a good idea, but I did pick Valerie up and sit with Olivia. Picking Valerie up was not easy, with all the wires attached to her for feeding and monitoring, and I needed to have a nurse help me safely position my baby in my arms. I wished I could just hold and hug Valerie without all the obstructions.

We then went over to my in-laws in the evening, as I did not want Olivia to miss having a normal Thanksgiving dinner. My in-laws were glad to see all of us, but they commented on how much weight my husband and I had lost due to the stressful situation.

I had dinner with the family, but after about two hours, I came back to the hospital to stay with Valerie afterwards, as I did not want to leave Valerie alone in the hospital during the holiday.

Valerie was evaluated by the hospital cardiac surgical team and her cardiologist after Thanksgiving. They decided she was stable enough for discharge to home with close outpatient follow-up. I was very nervous about that because I am not a doctor or a nurse and Valerie was still in such a precarious state. There was so much that she would need that I was unable to provide.

Chapter Eight

COMING HOME

The hospital gave me a checklist of all the things I needed to do—or learn—before I could safely take care of Valerie at home. I would need to be trained in infant cardiopulmonary resuscitation (CPR), as would anyone who would help me take care of her.

The hospital had been planning to send Valerie home without an oxygen tank, but I was very concerned about what would happen if she ran into difficulties. I requested oxygen and they agreed that it was probably a good idea. I also requested an oximeter, which assesses the oxygen saturation in the patient's blood so that I would know if there was a problem. Initially, I was informed that I'd be able to tell if Valerie needed oxygen; she would turn black and blue. But I was worried about what might happen if I was asleep or even if I just stepped out of Valerie's room to go to the bathroom. I wanted something to monitor her breathing at all times. I also needed to learn how to use a pulse oximeter because it was important to rotate it from legs to hands, to give her little body a break. I was relieved to have all this equipment, but getting it meant that I had to learn how to use it—how to put a nasal cannula on my little girl, how to turn the oxygen tank on, and what to do if we ran into any problems with the machinery. They gave me the nasal cannula, but I later decided that I really needed an infant oxygen mask, so I got one of those on my own.

In the end, it turned out that the oximeter caused a lot of chaos. Every time Valerie's oxygen level dipped a little—which it did very often—the oximeter would beep and wake the whole house. Often, though, I just needed to watch Valerie as the problem corrected itself. But I decided that it was better to know about every little blip in her oxygen saturation than to miss an event that would require me to use the oxygen tank. As annoying as it was during the night, I figured it was better to be safe than sorry.

I needed to learn how to assess whether she needed oxygen, and then how to use the machinery to give it to her when necessary. I called the Fire Department, as well as the gas and electric companies, to let them know that we had an oxygen tank in the house. We would need priority service if there were ever a power or telephone outage, in case Valerie needed oxygen.

Any movement, even coughing or crying, would cause her

oxygen levels to drop, because her heart was beating faster.

When she came home, Valerie was regularly receiving six different medications. I needed to learn all of them, including the proper dosages, side effects, and how to tell whether the medication is working; I needed to learn what to do if we missed a dose and I needed to develop a system to track everything because each medication had its own complicated schedule. I also had to keep an eye out for diarrhea and reflux, which were common side effects for some of the drugs Valerie was taking.

I also needed to learn all about the NG feeding tube. The hospital nurses trained me in checking the tube, priming it, fortifying the breast milk, inserting the food, and cleaning it out afterward. They even gave me a stethoscope so I could listen to Valerie's chest and check that the NG tube was properly in place. I also had to learn all about how much food Valerie needed and on what schedule. Each feeding took two hours to run, and we needed to feed Valerie every three hours. When I needed to give Valerie medicine, I first had to flush the milk out and then flush the medication through the tube.

I had to keep careful records of everything I did—from when I gave her food and medication, to any difficulties with oxygen or anything else, as well as her bowel movements and how often I changed her diapers. I also had to listen to Valerie's heart.

Even simple things like bathing Valerie were complicated by

her medical condition. The feeding bag was attached to the NG tube, which was inserted through her nose, so it was not easy to pick her up. I could not submerge her in water to bathe her, so I had to clean her by means of sponge baths and wiping.

Everything was complicated with a sick preemie, even the process of getting her home. I was happy—but nervous—about bringing her home. To begin with, Valerie was barely five pounds and infant car seats require the babies to weigh at least five pounds. If she dipped below that, we would have to get a special preemie car seat.

I was also concerned about the house. We were having problems with our new house. The contractor had left at the worst possible time. We were hoping that we would be able to take Valerie home soon, but the house was in no shape for a sick infant. I had to enlist my family from New Jersey to help put the house in reasonable order.

We had decided to renovate the entire house. We also added new hardwood floors throughout the house, replaced the leaky roof, and put in a new kitchen. On the outside, we replaced the garage door, rebuilt the deck, changed all the windows, and repaved the driveway.

I had originally hoped to complete the work little by little. But my husband spoke with the contractor and decided to get all the projects—all the mess—over with at one time. The plan was to do all the work at once—and get it out of the way. I think the huge project was sort of a distraction for my husband, so he would not have to spend all his time worrying about Valerie.

That plan would have been fine, had our contractor kept to the schedule. Unfortunately, the contractor quit, leaving the house half painted, three of the bathrooms untiled, and the bathroom sinks not installed. Instead of having everything in perfect order, as we had hoped, it was much more of a mess than before. And now Valerie was coming home.

Fortunately, our family came in from New Jersey and really helped us get everything in order—not fully completed, but totally functional. I even ordered a special elevated bed, like the kind Valerie had in the hospital.

Valerie was discharged at 1:00 p.m. on December 1. I loved being able to bring her home finally and finally getting her out of the hospital environment. I knew that having her home would boost all of our spirits, most importantly hers. I got her home within about a half hour. The hospital sent all of the supplies that day as well. So when Valerie and I pulled up to the house, the NG tube and all the feeding supplies and the oxygen tank and oximeter were all there waiting for us.

Walking her from the car to the house was exciting for both of us. This was the first time Valerie had ever been outside: the first time she had ever seen a tree or grass, the first time she had ever felt the sun on her face or breeze on her arm. I only wish it had not been such a cold December day; she could have enjoyed the outdoors a little more otherwise.

In the end, we decided to bury Valerie outside, so she would be surrounded by nature, by the outdoors that she did not get to experience much when she was alive. We wanted her to have that experience, at least after she was gone.

Fortunately, I would not be doing all this alone. I would have the assistance of home health nurses for part of the time. Most of these women were licensed practical nurses. Initially, we were only approved for six hours a day of assistance but eventually the health insurance company increased that to eight hours, then to twelve hours and finally up to sixteen hours a day. Initially, I had the aides come during the day so I could supervise them and keep an eye on everything. But after a while, I realized that I did have to sleep sometime, so I changed the schedule to have them come at night.

The home health nurse and her manager met us at the house when I brought Valerie home, to help us set up the room. It was really helpful to have them around because we had so many boxes of supplies that it was overwhelming.

After that day, we had a home health nurse, initially for four hours a day. While it was a tremendous help to have trained professionals assist me in caring for Valerie, it was also a lot of work. Every time we got a new nurse, I had to train her. There was a lot of turnover, too. Part of it was my fault; when I switched from daytime to nighttime care, I got a different nurse. Also, when the insurance company increased the number of hours we could have assistance, it usually meant a different or additional nurses, whom I would also have to train.

The nurses also did not know how to change Valerie's nasogastric tube. They did not have the skills to replace it if it became dislodged or to deal with the routine monthly replacement of the tube. I had to learn how to do this task myself. The alternative would have been to take Valerie to the emergency room every time there was a problem with the tube.

Valerie was on six different medications. They had to be delivered, via the nasogastric tube, at different times. I had a schedule posted for the nurses to follow, based on the hospital's instructions. Unfortunately, the nurses did not all understand the appropriate dosage for such a tiny child. Valerie was prescribed miniscule doses. We had to measure them with a small syringe. Due to the size of the syringe and their inexperience with nursing children, some of the nurses thought that the appropriate dosage was a full syringe, when actually the syringe should only have been filled to the first line.

We ran into some problems because of the weather. It was a rough winter and snowstorms sometimes meant that nurses could not get to our house in time for their shifts—or sometimes they could not get to us at all. It was also difficult during the holidays because nurses often took vacation around Christmas and New Year's Day. If the nurse did not arrive, I would call the home health service and let them know and they would try to find someone else to come and assist. There were days when I was left alone to care for Valerie.

It also turned out that many home health nurses are accustomed to working with elderly patients. They do not know everything that has to be done with a pediatric patient. Eventually I realized that I could advocate for Valerie and arrange for home health nurses who had experience with babies, but unfortunately, it took me a while to figure that out.

Ultimately, the home care nurses were a mixed blessing. We went through five nurses in the short time Valerie was home. There were two memorable ones with whom we still keep in touch. Maureen and Grace had many years of experience and understood the severity of Valerie's condition. They also showed sensitivity and compassion toward our family. And they both wholeheartedly loved Valerie. The other nurses, unfortunately, worked part time and were not well prepared to deal with our situation.

I cannot imagine how other families who do not speak English or do not have the time to question their insurance companies cope. In talking to other mothers with an HLHS child, I realized that I was very lucky. One mother did not get any home care nursing help until a year later and her child was just as ill as Valerie. I did not know how some of them survived in a situation like that with no financial help. How did they manage to get their bills paid?

Chapter Nine

'TIS THE SEASON

While the weather did cause problems, the Christmas season was just the season for Valerie's return, a time full of family and celebrations. We got to enjoy Valerie at home during the Christmas and New Year holidays. It was such a blessing to be together over the holidays. We decided to stay home for the holidays and invite everyone to visit us. I could never have asked for a better Christmas present than my little girl. Having the whole family together rejoicing was exactly what we all needed to keep the hope strong in our lives. We all got full on holiday meals and bonded with our new bundle in the way that we needed at that time.

I closed off Valerie's room from the family, hoping to keep her safe from the winter colds and viruses that often ran rampant. But even though Valerie was not out in the living room with all the relatives, everyone—including Olivia—stopped by her room to say hello and see how she was doing. A lot of friends sent Christmas tree ornaments engraved with Valerie's name, which was very sweet. I was particularly happy when her paternal grandfather and uncle stopped by because they were both pediatricians. They knew how to interact with a sick baby and were able to assess her condition and give me some information.

My brother-in-law wanted to take photographs on Christmas Day to immortalize the gift of Valerie. I started to put Valerie into her fancy clothes, so she would look especially lovely for the photos, but her oxygen levels started fluctuating and I had to stop. I checked her oxygen level with the oximeter and ended up having to give her oxygen on Christmas Day. I was glad that I'd been fully trained and was able to do that without having to call the hospital for help. But I was not able to bring Valerie downstairs that day for photographs.

My brother-in-law took photos of Valerie upstairs in my arms, in her father's arms, and with her sister Olivia. Olivia was smiling particularly broadly in those photos and it makes me happy to look at them and remember how excited Olivia was.

At one point, I quickly took out the NG tube from Valerie's nose so that we could take a few photos without the obstruction. I only had about ten minutes before I had to reinsert it, but we were able to get a few photographs. My favorite is the one with Olivia.

That picture, in fact, ended up being the only one we were able to take with our two daughters and no hospital equipment.

Olivia's favorite cousin, Ava, came to visit. Ava was eight years old at that point, a little older than Olivia, but the two of them got along like sisters. Ava was an only child, so she appreciated playing with a little cousin.

Ava became very attached to Valerie as well. She wrote a poem for Valerie and sang a song to the family. She sang it to the tune of Rachel Platten's 2014 song, "***This Is My Fight Song***."

This is my fight song

Take back my life song

Prove I'm all right song

My power's turned on . . .

Ava felt that the lyrics fit Valerie perfectly; she was fighting for her life, fighting to stay here, with her family and friends. Ava sang it to my family, dedicating it to Valerie.

We decided to stay home for New Year's Eve and New Year's Day, too, even though we traditionally went to our in-laws for the day. We decided it was a little thing to give up, to have the pleasure of Valerie's company. Again, people came to visit and it was lovely to have everyone around. Everyone was happy to see Valerie in our new home.

Olivia was thrilled to have her sister home, finally. But I had to keep Olivia from Valerie's room as much as possible. I was afraid that even if Olivia was perfectly healthy, she might be carrying germs from school, and Valerie was so vulnerable to any kind of infection. I had Olivia stand at the door to Valerie's room and talk to her from there.

Olivia drew pictures for Valerie, mostly colorful flowers, which I hung by Valerie's bed. And she always wanted to touch Valerie, at least a little, like her hair or her toes.

In addition to her heart problems, Valerie was already beginning to manifest some of the other symptoms of Wolf-Hirschhorn syndrome. She was starting to have liver problems, which was noticed while she was in the hospital.

Despite all the work and all the problems I had to deal with, I was glad to have Valerie home from the hospital. Our respite did not last long, however, and before I knew it we were back at the hospital.

On the morning of January 7, Valerie was really fussy. She had more frequent stools than usual that night, and her pulse oximeter was reading abnormal numbers. I kept changing her and trying to cheer her up. But I was in a panic because I could not figure out how to help her stop crying. Then I noticed that Valerie's oxygen level had fallen to 50 percent. The pulse oximeter kept fluctuating up and down and up and down. She started turning blue, which made me even more worried.

At seven o'clock in the morning, I called the hospital and the pediatric cardiologist on call said that Valerie might be getting sick, perhaps a bad cold. I asked whether I should bring her into the hospital and the doctor said he thought it would be a good idea. He recommended we use an ambulance so that she could start receiving care as soon as the vehicle pulled up, rather than waiting until she got to the hospital.

The hospital examined Valerie and recommended that she be brought back for surgery the next day. Because of the problems with her circulatory system, her lungs were full of fluid. The slow blood flow from the left side of her heart had resulted in blood pooling in and creating pressure in her left atrium. The doctors planned to do another balloon septostomy. This time, the doctors hoped that enlarging the hole between her atria again would decompress her left atrium and alleviate the congestion in her lungs.

I called an ambulance, but I was worried about the snow. We had experienced a snowstorm a few days earlier and the accumulation was very high. We live on a sloping hill and, between the unpaved driveway, the tremendous amount of snow, and the acute slant of the driveway, the ambulance had a difficult time reaching the house.

Eventually the ambulance driver gave up trying to drive to our front door, and two EMS workers got out of the ambulance to carry Valerie to the vehicle. They slipped and slid their way to the house—and then back to the ambulance with Valerie in their arms.

I got into the ambulance with Valerie and my husband took Olivia in our car to the hospital. The EMS workers checked Valerie and she had a slight fever.

Chapter Ten

THE DAY VALERIE DIED

The procedure the next day, on January 8, was supposed to be simple, but it turned out to be quite difficult and took a lot longer than usual. We believed so strongly that she would fight her way out of it, as she had done before. After all, why wouldn't she? She had been a strong fighter so far; couldn't she go the rest of the way and make it out even stronger? I wanted nothing more than that. It was supposed to be a simple procedure, and after pulling through all the other times, we did not think that Valerie would not make it this time.

Dr. T., the pediatric cardiologist, completed the balloon septostomy, which he had performed once before on Valerie. But unlike the last time, it took him over four hours. The nurses finally brought Valerie back to the intensive care room to go into recovery. When Valerie was transferred back to the PICU, I felt uneasy, as Valerie looked so exhausted. I expressed my concern to the nurses and doctor, but the plan was to extubate her shortly afterwards, removing the endotracheal tube.

It was about 5:00 p.m., and my husband and I were tired. My husband's parents dropped Olivia off at the hospital and I told my husband to go eat with her. I did not want to leave Valerie, as something told me to stay. My husband decided to just grab food from the cafeteria with Olivia and stayed at the hospital too. He got me some food and told me to come out to eat in the waiting room. As I was about to step out, Valerie opened her eyes and looked at me (the last time she ever opened her eyes). It was very odd, because she had just come out of surgery, was heavily drugged, and still had a breathing tube in her throat.

As she closed her eyes, her heart rate jumped. I called for the nurse and PICU doctor. Her heart was beating far too fast and its rhythm was fluctuating. I went to the waiting room and asked my husband to come in, as the doctor was starting to throw around a lot of terms, which he could better understand than me. Almost an hour later, waiting in the waiting room with Olivia, I got nervous and texted my husband. He did not answer the phone. I could not leave Olivia, so I called my mother-in-law to see if she could come to watch Olivia. She sent my brother-in-law and his wife, who lived nearby, to the hospital. As they got there, I ran into Valerie's room. I saw a line of nurses taking turns to perform CPR on

Valerie. My heart dropped. I stood there for a moment and broke down. I ran out of the room so angry that my husband has not told me. He ran after me and said he did not want me to see her like that. I calmed down and went back in. I looked at her and I just did not want them to continue. She was too tired and I just did not want her to be in any more pain. But my body froze and like a deer in headlights, I did not say anything.

Dr. T. had completed the balloon spectostomy; however, unfortunately, Valerie went into metabolic acidosis, a condition in which too much acid builds up in the blood. Although it has a number of causes, metabolic acidosis can be caused by cardiac issues. The metabolic acidosis led to an arrhythmia (or irregular heartbeat) and ultimately to heart failure. Valerie began having periodic blocked heartbeats, in which individual heartbeats began, as they usually do, in the right atrium, but failed to reach the ventricles, or lower chambers of the heart, as they should. The frequency of blocked heartbeats increased and her baseline heart rate decreased. She was also starting to get heart blockages.

Atropine was given in the hopes that it would increase Valerie's heart rate and to help with the blockages, but it had no effect. Chest compressions and doses of epinephrine were given to help sustain her heart rate. Gradually the pacer output was increased to the maximum dose, but that was stopped for inefficacy. My husband and I were asked to leave Valerie's room, as Dr. T., the cardiologist, was called in to place a transvenous pacer wire, a type of temporary pacemaker inserted through the veins. After twenty minutes, they called us back in and said that there was no longer any indication that the heart muscles were contracting. Compressions were stopped and Valerie was placed in my arm to pass.

As much as I hated the thought of it, little Valerie lost her fight. There was nothing any of us could do to stop it. The fight was over for all of us. She passed on January 8, 2015, at 11:30 p.m. It is a date that I will remember for the rest of my life.

After she passed, I sat holding Valerie with the greatest despair, beyond words. Dr. T. approached me and gave his condolences. He told me to say goodbye and to know that there was so much love in the room for our whole family. However, I was zoned out and the only thing that I heard, which I am upset about still, is that their goal from the day Valerie was born was only to let us bring her home to enjoy. It was never to actually save her from this illness. I know he was speaking the truth, but I did not want to hear that, at least not at that time. Meanwhile, my goal was always to see her grow old and fight against her illness. That is, to successfully walk away from the three-part major heart repair that she would have had to go through if she had lived. Perhaps my hope was not realistic. But it is a mother's job to be a child's biggest advocate. That is, to support and provide unconditional love every step of the way.

My husband and I asked the nurse to sew Valerie back up, as they had to make an incision during the attempt to place the transvenous pacer wire. We pulled out her IV lines and dressed her with clothes from home. I layered her with a bodysuit, hat, socks, and gloves because Valerie hates the cold. I brushed her hair and cleaned her face and hands. Valerie looked bloated/inflated, with rosy cheeks, but most of all she looked peaceful, pain-free, and relieved.

Valerie fought hard to live; that much I did know. I had never known a stronger fighter than the one in that little body of hers. She wanted more than anything to stay with us and live a long life. She did not deserve to die before she even got the chance to live. I wanted that for her to and wish I could have given it to her.

The experience was harrowing for all of us. We knew everything that Valerie went through. We felt all her pain from all the different procedures that she underwent. It is something no parent or child should ever have to endure. As a parent, whether you like it or not, you feel the pain that your child experiences. Unfortunately, sometimes bad things just happen and we cannot do anything about it.

Valerie had to struggle with every breath, but she survived procedure after procedure and crisis after crisis. This time, however, our fighter was not strong enough and she had to leave our life to go off to a better one. She was with us three months, sixteen days, and six hours of her life. It was the best three and half months we could have ever had with her and I am blessed to have had her even for that long.

She is a special baby, and knowing that she is taken care of by God is comforting. Knowing that Valerie bears no pain brings me a lot of joy. There are no more operating rooms for her. She is in heaven now, enjoying herself. She can do whatever she wants without worrying about a weak heart. In heaven, she can be as free and healthy as can be. She can be the Valerie she was always meant to be, and that thought alone kept me happy. I just want her to be okay, to know true happiness. It was a difficult time, but there were voices from the Angels every time I missed her, whispering to me that Valerie is in heaven. Those whispers brought me peace.

Chapter Eleven

THE VIEWING BEFORE THE FUNERAL

The viewing was about a week after Valerie's death, on January 16 at 9:00 a.m. at the Christ the Redeemer Catholic Church in Sterling, Virginia. Father Patrick, who baptized Valerie in the hospital, was going to perform the funeral Mass that morning for her as well. We were very close to him; he is a wonderful priest that prayed for Valerie throughout her stay in the hospital. We are blessed to have him be part of our lives and our journey. We called him at odd hours and he came to the hospital to pray for Valerie. We could not ask for a better man of God to be with us during our time of need. He also suggested that we use the Adams Green Funeral Home. The people who worked there were really nice and empathetic.

When things got under way, our families gathered around. It was so wonderful to have everyone together like that. It made me feel that everyone has so much love for Valerie and our family. I desperately needed the support of my family during that time. Some of my family came from New Jersey the night before for the viewing, and the majority of my family came the morning of the funeral. They all wanted to be there to pay their respects to Valerie and to also say goodbye. The viewing the night before was tiny, with only a few relatives in attendance. My family did not come until late that night. My husband's family did not come at all.

The next day would be the day that I would say goodbye to Valerie, even though I knew she would always be with us in spirit. It would not be an easy day to say the least and anyone who has experienced the loss of a child will understand that there is nothing like that sort of loss. I felt the same way that I did when my cousin had died: funerals . . . I hate funerals. I prayed to God, to my cousin Hong, and everyone who I know passed away. I asked them to take care of Valerie for me.

It was the first time I saw Valerie again after her death at the hospital on the night of January 8. The funeral home dressed her up in a white gown that I had given them. I had chosen the dress that my daughter Olivia was baptized in, as it would be a gift from her big sister. I knew she would look like a beautiful little Angel. I was right; she looked beautiful and like the Angel I always knew she would be.

Valerie also wore a hat that the hospital had given to us from a foundation that makes Angel gowns for stillborn babies and infant burials from donated wedding gowns. Unfortunately, the gown was too small for Valerie and I only took the hat. I tried contacting the foundation to donate my wedding gown afterwards, but they said there was a surplus of gowns donated and for me to hold off on sending my gown.

I was there with my husband, my sister Oanh, my brother Khuong, and his wife Nga. Together we prayed for her, like we had done a thousand times before that. Praying for Valerie made me feel that much closer to her. We had prayer but mostly, we found peace through her angelic face. I could stare at that little face all night if I could. She had been such a huge part of our lives even though she was not with us for very long. Looking down at her tears just filled my eyes. So peaceful, porcelain-like, Angel . . .

That night, when we went home, we found that we could still smell Valerie in the house. Her crib and blanket had the same funeral home smell that her body had. I felt her presence in our house and knew that she was still with us. I gathered her favorite music mobile that we had placed over her crib, some clothes, hats, socks, mittens, and toys so that I can bring them to the funeral the next morning to be buried with her.

Chapter Twelve

VALERIE'S FUNERAL

The morning viewing started at 9:00 a.m. Family and friends from near and far came trickling in to give their condolences. My family alone from New Jersey was about forty people and my husband's coworkers, friends and family were just as many. I stood by Valerie's side the entire morning, while my husband greeted the guests.

My husband and I picked a tiny coffin for Valerie, no more than two feet long. This way she could be buried with other kids in Baby Land, which did not permit coffins any larger. In fact, most coffins in Baby Land were the size of a shoe box. We picked the largest size for Valerie because we wanted her to be comfortable and we wanted to be able to bury a number of things with her.

She looked peaceful and Angel-like. I took off my gold

diamond necklace cross, which my husband had given me during my baptism many years ago, and put it on Valerie to be buried. I wanted her to take that with her to heaven so she would be protected by God. My husband would look for the same necklace every time he passed a jewelry store. I told him to not bother, as certain things can never be replaced and if we can find the same one again, then it is because Valerie wants to give it back to me. For now, part of my heart is with her and I am happy that way.

The Mass started at 11:00 a.m., right on schedule as expected. My brother picked up Olivia at home and brought her to the Mass, as I did not want Olivia, as a three-year-old, to see her sister in a coffin at the viewing. The coffin was now covered, so Olivia could not see Valerie. But somehow, Olivia kept looking at it and I could see in her eyes that she knew Valerie was in there.

The process was the same for most funerals: a gathering, then the Liturgy of the Word, Liturgy of the Eucharist, and then the eulogy. Father Patrick allowed us to say a few words, even though a eulogy is not normally given at Catholic masses, because, he said, people can go on and on forever. Afterwards, he commended us for the short and yet inspiring eulogy.

It was my husband's job to do the eulogy and I knew that it was going to be hard on him. We expect men to be the strong ones, like stone walls, but men crumble too, especially when it comes to a loss of their child. One minute they could be strong and the next they fall apart sobbing with tears.

My husband asked me to walk up with him for the eulogy. I needed to be there for him as much as I needed him to be there for me; I would take care of him as he would take care of me. We walked up there together as a united front. But once he got on the stage, he could not go through with it. He broke down sobbing in front of everyone and could not deliver the eulogy. It broke my heart seeing him like that, so broken and lost over the death of our little girl. The pain was excruciating but I knew that we would get through it and move on. We did not have any other choice but to accept her death. I took over and read the eulogy for him. My husband had written it and put so much thought and feeling into what we wanted to say.

Eulogy:
We named her after Saint Valerie
Valiant, strong, courageous
Because we knew she would need to be, to survive

And she did
She made it to full term
She made it through the first surgery, then the second, then
the third surgery, then the fourth
She was intubated 6 times, every single time she tried to fight
her way out

Angels Bloom

We felt her pain with every single scar on her body

Saw her struggle with every single breath

And she pulled through over and over

She wanted to live

She fought to live

She wanted to be with her mother

And her sister, Olivia

Olivia, her three-year-old sister told us yesterday

"Valerie loves me"

I said, "How do you know?"

"Because she looked at me, she loves me"

She gave us 3 months, 16 days, and 6 hours of her life

We know she is in heaven now

Running, playing, laughing, and smiling

And most of all pain free . . .

We thank everyone for being here

We thank everyone for their thoughts and prayers

We know everyone has been asking what they can do to help

The one thing we should have done more of

You can help—by spending a little more time with your son

or daughter when possible

Angels Bloom

Hug them a little more

Walk with them a little more

Talk to them a little more

We think Valerie will like that

Valerie—Daddy loves you, Mama loves you, and Olivia loves you

Thank you.

Family and friends followed us to the National Memorial Park Cemetery in Falls Church, Virginia, where Valerie was buried. We chose to bury her with other kids her age. In fact, Valerie is one of the oldest infant there, being three months old. The plot is called Baby Land, shaped like a heart. It was extremely cold, windy, and dreary that day, recovering from the week's long snow and rain. After the burial, our family and friends came over to our house for a late lunch, which we catered. I just wanted to go to bed at that point, so I took some alcoholic beverages to knock me out until the next morning.

Chapter Thirteen

THE LOVE BETWEEN SISTERS

It is hard to decide what another child should have to endure when it comes to a death of a sibling. We had to discuss whether or not Olivia would attend the wake or the funeral. Death was upsetting enough without throwing a small child into a funeral full of grief. On the day of Valerie's funeral, we only let Olivia attend the Mass and not the viewing and the burial. We were not sure if she could handle it at her age and did not want to put any added stress on her. We just believed that the viewing would be too much for her. She attended the Mass and was able to pay her respects to Valerie in her own way; then my sister took her home. I was not quite sure how she processed everything that went on around her but children are resilient and I knew she would be okay.

While in the car, my sister told Olivia that Valerie is in heaven now. Olivia replied, "No, she is still with us." The comment surprised my sister and I too was surprised when my sister told me. When Olivia made the comment, Olivia looked over into my car and gazed at the back seat. Olivia insisted that Valerie is with us. Was it possible that Valerie was in the car with us, in spirit? As an Angel, watching over us? I truly believe that it was possible and that maybe only Olivia could see her.

Once the ceremony ended we all went from the church to the cemetery for the burial. It was a quiet time for us and the air around us was still. It had rained a few days before, so the graveside was really wet. The sound of sloshing feet throughout the graveside was heard all around us. The rain and cloudiness around us made the experience that much more depressing and dreary. Not that you expect a day like that to be warm and sunny— after all a sweet child is being put to rest—but I still did not like the rain. It made me feel cold right down to my bones. Or maybe that feeling had nothing to do with the rain at all. Watching my daughter be buried was more than enough to make me feel cold. When it came time for the burial, they had to scoop out buckets of water before the casket was lowered. The sight of it was creepy. Everyone sat patiently as this was done; buckets of water were coming out of the grave, and all the while we all knew what was going to be lowered into it. We all just sat in silence and watched as it happened and nobody ever talked about it afterwards. It was almost surreal to watch the goings-on of getting the grave ready for her casket to be lowered.

But somehow Olivia knew about it even though no one spoke to her about it. A few months after, she sat one day and told me that she missed Valerie. It was a hard conversation to have but both my husband and I knew exactly how she felt. To my surprise Olivia said, "They put her in a box, Mama. And it was wet. She did not like it because it was wet." I did not connect right away and asked her what she meant. Olivia repeated it again and said that was what Valerie told her. The thought that it could be true that my daughter could have said those words shook me to my core. Not only that but it hurt my heart to think that Valerie did not like the wet grave. The wet grass, the wet grave, and most of all, the wet box we had put her to rest in. "She did not like it because it was wet." My poor little baby Angel Valerie.

Chapter Fourteen

PLAY AREA

I was relieved to have the funeral over with. After the funeral, my family stayed at our house for a few days with us. I enjoyed having everyone together, bonding together once again. One day my brother, Tri, was playing with his daughter Victoria, my other niece Ava, and Olivia. They were in Olivia's kitchen play area pretending to cook and eat.

Olivia was pretending to take orders and she said to my brother, "Okay, I will take orders for the five of us." Confused, my brother said, "There are only four of us. Me, you, Victoria, and Ava." Olivia said, "No, there are five of us. Me, you, Victoria, Ava, and Blah Blah." Mumbling the last name. My brother said, "Are you sure?" And Olivia said, "Yes. There are five of us," and repeated the same names again, mumbling the fifth name. My brother asked, "Who is Blah Blah?" Olivia looked at him and just smiled. My brother did not know what to make of it. Who was the fifth person?

Ava was very affected by Valerie's passing and mentioned it in several diary entries in early 2015. On February 7, she wrote: "I am writing because on January 9 or 8 my little cousin Valerie died. I have so much sorrow in my heart and very sad. But I got to live life." Ava signed this entry: "Sad and happy."

Then, a little more than a month later, Ava wrote another diary entry: "I miss Valerie so much. I wanted to show Olivia how to be like an older sister. Valerie was a very strong baby, her name means strong, and that is what she is. She made it in her last surgery but she was too weak after so she died. I love her. She and Olivia are my sisters because I love them like one. I only saw her once but in my heart I know she loves me and that she is in heaven with God." Ava signed this entry with a large heart and the word "love."

Chapter Fifteen

PINK ELEPHANT

A few days after the funeral, the funeral home mailed all the Mass cards and sympathy cards, the sign-in book, and the stuffed animals, which were given to us the day of the funeral. Within the things mailed back, there was a pink elephant that was left right next to Valerie's open casket, which as you remember Olivia never saw. Coincidentally, also arriving in the mail the same day were some toys and stuffed animals from a friend of ours, in an effort to cheer Olivia up. All the items were placed together in the kitchen.

Olivia came home from prekindergarten that day and I told her that she had some gifts from our friends. Of course Olivia loved stuffed animals just like any other child would. When she saw them she was so excited she grabbed the toys and stuffed animals. She then grabbed the pink elephant and said, "All of the other toys

82

are mine, but this pink elephant belongs to Valerie."

I was shocked because out of all the toys and stuffed animals, how could she know that the pink elephant specifically belonged to Valerie? It puzzled me that she said such a thing. I turned to her and asked her why she said that. She told me that she just knew that it belonged to Valerie. There was no possible way for her to know that and yet she had this look on her face that said otherwise. She just smiled, as I questioned her again. I could not have been more confused about the words that were coming out of her mouth.

There is a Buddhist belief that souls stay with their families for seven weeks, or forty-nine days, after the body passes, to visit with the family. We also believe that children—like Olivia—can see these souls because their eyes are still naïve and trusting.

I believe that Valerie has visited with us over this time. Olivia saw her when she set a place for Valerie in the make-believe kitchen, and again when she told us that the pink elephant belonged to Valerie. Similarly, there was another time when my sister came to visit and Olivia sang her a few songs. My husband and I noticed that the three songs she sang were from Valerie's swing music. Simultaneously, we both intuited that Valerie was singing through Olivia. Then, suddenly, Olivia's picture frame fell down onto the dresser; no one was near it nor did anyone bump anything. It was as though Valerie was confirming what my husband and I had been thinking.

And Olivia was not the only child who could see Valerie after she passed. The week after the funeral, my brother, his wife, and their daughter Victoria, my niece, who was then two years old, spent the night in Olivia's bedroom. Victoria had a hard time getting to sleep. She kept looking at the bedroom door and crying. Finally, my brother said, "Valerie, if that is you, then please do not bother Victoria. Let her go to sleep now." Immediately—and with no warning—Victoria laid down and fell right to sleep. She slept peacefully through the rest of the night.

I wondered whether all these thoughts of Valerie lingering around the house were all in my imagination, because of my desperate desire for her to be around. However, there was a time after Valerie's death that I had difficulty deciphering my dreams— not understanding them, just trying to figure out whether what I had seen in my sleep had really happened or had occurred only in a dream. My husband told me that he'd seen this before, that it was a natural part of the grieving process. Possibly there is a defense mechanism in your body that you use to protect yourself. The loss of Valerie was overwhelming for my body mentally and physically. Remembering what the Angel told me through the valet helps. That is, that this life was too hard for Valerie but soon God would give me another one, one who was better suited to this world. Indeed, that did happen and Isabella was given to us. Isabella's birth helped me emotionally, and it also caused a spiritual awakening, as I saw the all-consuming importance of hope. It was then, when I realized the gift of Isabella, that I started to develop my belief in Angels.

Chapter Sixteen

ACCEPTANCE AND HOPE

We were invited to the hospital remembrance ceremony, called the Pediatric Ceremony of Remembrance, which was intended to honor all the babies who passed over the previous year. We were not sure whether to go or not. We thought it might be difficult to be in that place, with those people who held such painful memories for us. But we also did not know whether we would feel that we missed something important if we stayed home. And we would never know what we might have gained from the ceremony. My husband said the decision was up to me and so I decided, with great trepidation, that we would attend, all three of us.

If we had not been worried that the ceremony would be sad, it was clarified for us quickly. We got in line to check in and the hospital staff started handing out tissue boxes to each attendee.

My husband and I were right. In attendance, in addition to all the parents and family members of the children, were a number of doctors and other staff from the NICU. We saw the surgeon who operated on Valerie as well as some of the nurses who had taken care of her.

They offered appetizers and, after we mingled for a little bit, the hospital staff handed out pieces of paper and pencils and asked us to write down a message that we wanted to send to our child. There was a tree in the room covered with origami paper cranes and they hung each note on a crane. There is a belief that cranes bring messages to heaven.

At this point, I was three months pregnant. I was glad to be able to share my good news with the doctors and nurses in attendance. I also told them that I was getting excellent care and even had an echocardiogram and both baby and mother were fine.

I made a point to talk with the hospital chaplain, who had been a great source of comfort while Valerie was fighting for her life. The chaplain would often come up to me and ask whether I wanted to say a prayer. I always did. She, too, was pleased to hear about my pregnancy.

We also spoke with one of the pediatric intensivists (Dr. Stephen) who had worked with Valerie. This gentleman was a friend of the family and was very kind at the remembrance ceremony. He told us that Valerie was very special and that we had been good parents. This connection, incidentally, is one of the reasons my husband had wanted Valerie to continue treatment at this hospital, rather than switch to a facility farther away.

At the end of the evening, everyone who had written a message to a child got the note itself and the crane it hung from to take home.

After that event, our family was invited to Valerie's remembrance ceremony at Christ the Redeemer Church. The ceremony, which took place on November 10, was designed to honor all of the people who had passed in the previous year. Each of the families received a rose. We got one in memory of Valerie. I brought the rose home and put it in a vase. To our surprise, the rose survived for more than two months around Christmas. Not only was the rose alive, it shot out a baby bulb. I did some research and this does happen to roses, but very rarely—and not without special care. We did not actually take particularly good care of the rose. We cut off the baby bulb and put the stem is a pot of soil hoping that the rose would stay alive.

My husband decided that we should try to take special care of the baby bud, so we did some research on the Internet and learned that we should put it in a potato because potatoes provide just the right amount of nutrients and moisture for a little rose.

Unfortunately, the baby rose died around Christmas and New Year's, just around when Valerie passed away.

After Valerie died, I spent a lot of time thinking about her. I realized that I really wanted to know how she was doing in heaven. I believe she is no longer sick and in pain, and she knows that we love and miss her. And I'm sure she knows that she will see us all again one day. I believe that Valerie was a special soul and an Angel who came to us as a gift.

Since then, I have given birth to another little girl, Isabella. She was born in excellent health, and weighed six pounds, eight ounces and measured twenty inches long. My husband and I were very happy—and relieved.

My husband and his relatives think that Isabella looks very much like Valerie, and he believes that the reason is that Isabella has Valerie's soul. I cannot judge whether Isabella resembles Valerie; they are both beautiful in their own way.

Part of the reason he believes that is when Valerie was sick, he went to see a fortune-teller. The fortune-teller told him that we would have another child and that Valerie's soul would come back in that child.

I do not believe this. I believe that Valerie was a wonderful child, a beautiful soul, and that Isabelle, too, is a wonderful child with a beautiful soul—and that they are two different souls.

Both my husband and I believe that Valerie is an Angel that watches over the family. She observes us and when I talk to her inside my head, I feel like there is a voice that responds inside me and guides me through the day, helping me make decisions. And I believe this is Valerie. I am not saying that I hear voices, only that Valerie gives me a sense, when I am faced with a decision, of what is the right thing to do, the best way to go.

Olivia, too, misses Valerie and knows that her little sister is in heaven. One day, when we saw a dead bird outside our house, Olivia turned to me and said that the bird was up in heaven with Valerie.

I would like to encourage other parents who have lost a child to understand a few things about this great sadness.

First, I want you to commend mothers and fathers for all their tremendous efforts to save their children: for driving to the doctor and the hospital at all times of day and night and in all kinds of weather; for learning more than you ever wanted to know about health care and medicine; for juggling every other aspect of your life—family, work, home—to be able to truly be there for your ill child. You fight as hard as you can, but you have to know when to stop fighting.

The experience makes you a stronger person. I know that, for me, I am less afraid of death, because I know that day will come and I will be reunited with Valerie. Also, I know that I can go through the worst life has to offer. Surely there is nothing more painful than sitting in the hospital at two o'clock in the morning with your dead child in your arms. If you can survive that, I believe, you can survive anything. The strength that I gained through our experiences with Valerie makes everything else in life somehow easier.

I also believe that you learn that, at some point, you cannot dictate life. You can do the best that you possibly can, and then accept the situation and move on. Once you accept that some things are just out of your control, the challenges become less onerous. I am not saying that this is easy. It takes a very strong person to learn to accept the inevitable. And acceptance makes you a stronger person.

In my heart, I am aware that knowing God and the Angels are watching over me and my family makes it easier to accept. There is a reason for everything; we might not know it at the time, but it is important to believe. Talk to your Angels and they help you to accept, they will provide comfort and hope. Your Angels are within you and, as such, they are always with you, always watching. And the child that you lost is also an Angel looking out for you, helping you to move on, to achieve greater understanding and acceptance.

Chapter Seventeen

EMOTIONAL TRAUMA FROM LOSING A CHILD

Like I said before, living through the devastation of losing a child is something that no one can ever begin to understand unless they went through it too. It is the kind of situation that makes you feel completely lost and helpless. Even after burying your child it stays with you always no matter what you do. It lingers and follows you throughout your whole life. Even when time passes and you move on, you find yourself thinking about it. It hits you randomly and you find yourself feeling the loss over and over again throughout your life. The death of a child can affect your life in so many different ways; even in a loving marriage. Statistically, some marriages end in a divorce through the loss of a child. How we grieve is very different between men and woman. You need to learn to be there for each other through such a hard time. We almost need to learn to love each other again and grow from this experience.

The home care nurse warned me about this while Valerie was alive, warning me in advance. She said that many couples with heart-problem kids end up in a divorce. They blame each other for it happening to them. They are stressed over the situation and do not know how to handle it. Communication is so important during such a time. Most parents are exhausted for having to take care of a child twenty-four hours a day. They get burned out really easily and give up on each other.

The death of a child is considered one of the most difficult and traumatic events that a family can experience. It is a devastating, yet a unique experience for each individual of the family. Each year more than 300,000 children die in America, leaving thousands of families to cope with this tragedy.

The death of a child is a violation of the natural order of things. Parents expect their children to bury them, not to bury their children. Since this natural order has been disrupted, parents must now readapt to a new, seemingly illogical reality. In the Asian tradition, elders would often not attend a child's funeral.

Parents do not easily comprehend that even though they are older, the creator, the protector, and the provider of their child, they have still survived and their child has not. The young are to grow up and replace the old. The personal identity of each parent, which was tied to their child, has been changed as well as their behavior and lifestyle. They lose a part of their future and their posterity. Parents tend to feel impotent and to feel a great sense of remorse and guilt over not protecting their child from death. They feel so helpless that they were not able to protect their child or to prevent the death. The life of each parent is forever changed; the marital dyad is forever changed as well. There is a great need for each spouse to know how things need to be between them now.

I had all these feelings filter through me in the year after Valerie's passing. Valerie can never be replaced, but we did find comfort and support from family and friends. We have been blessed to have another baby girl just like the Angels told me.

RESOURCES

The following annotated list of useful resources can help you find out more in-depth information about a variety of medical and emotional topics. Please note, this is not an exhaustive list, rather simply a useful place to start.

Amniocentesis:

- American Pregnancy Association. This brief website outlines how and when doctors perform amniocentesis, the process of the procedure, and possible side effects. See **http://americanpregnancy.org/prenatal-testing/amniocentesis/.**

- Mayo Clinic. This webpage describes the procedure, purpose, and risks and outlines how to prepare and what to expect. See **http://www.mayoclinic.org/tests-procedures/amniocentesis/basics/definition/prc-20014529**.

- WebMD. Geared to new parents, this website discusses amniocentesis, its accuracy, risks, process, and results. See **http://www.webmd.com/baby/guide/amniocentesis**.

- Wikipedia. This encyclopedia entry explains the various approaches to determine the fetus's sex prior to birth. See **https://en.wikipedia.org/wiki/Amniocentesis**.

Arachnoid brain cysts:

- National Organization for Rare Disorders. This website describes arachnoid cysts and describes the signs and symptoms, causes, affected populations, and related disorders.

See **https://rarediseases.org/rare-diseases/arachnoid-cysts/**.

Cardiac catheterization:

- American Heart Association. This PDF focuses on pediatric therapeutic cardiac catheterization, detailing the various forms of sedation and the techniques involved. See **http://www.heart.org/idc/groups/heart-public/@wcm/@hcm/documents/downloadable/ucm_30 7680.pdf**.

- Journal of the American College of Cardiology. "Complications Associated with Pediatric Cardiac Catheterization." Geared to physicians, this academic article describes a study of the relative risks of pediatric diagnostic catheterization. See **http://content.onlinejacc.org/article.aspx?articleid=112 5460**.

- KidsHealth. This webpage outlines the diagnostic and treatment roles that pediatric catheterization can play. See **http://kidshealth.org/parent/medical/heart/cardiac_cath eter.html#**.

- University of North Carolina at Chapel Hill School of Medicine Department of Pediatrics. This webpage discusses how pediatric catheterization can replace the need for open-heart surgery. See **https://www.med.unc.edu/cmep/specialties/cardiology/p rocedures/pediatric-cardiac-catheterization**.

- WebMD. This section describes the process of heart catheterization. See **http://www.webmd.com/heart-disease/heart-catheterization-for-congenital-heart-defects**.

Contractility:

- The Free Dictionary. This dictionary entry provides a

definition of contractility. See **http://medical-dictionary.thefreedictionary.com/contractility**.

- Wikipedia. See **https://en.wikipedia.org/wiki/Contractility.**

Cysts in fetal brains:

- Contemporary Ob/Gyn. Geared to physicians, this webpage outlines the implications and outcomes of isolated fetal choroid plexus cysts. See **http://contemporaryobgyn.modernmedicine.com/contemporary-obgyn/content/tags/fetal-choroid-plexus-cysts/isolated-fetal-choroid-plexus-cysts.**

- Journal of Prenatal Medicine. "Fetal Intracranial Cysts: Prenatal Diagnosis and Outcome." This academic article discusses the importance of prenatal diagnosis for fetuses with cysts in the brain. See **http://www.ncbi.nlm.nih.gov/pmc/articles/PMC3279101/.**

- Journal of Ultrasound in Medicine. "Prenatal Diagnosis of a Suprasellar Arachnoid Cyst with 2- and 3-Dimensional Sonography and Fetal Magnetic Resonance Imaging: Difficulties in Management and Review of the Literature." This academic article reviews the literature on prenatal diagnosis of fetal brain cysts. See **http://www.jultrasoundmed.org/content/29/10/1487.full**

- Wikipedia. This encyclopedia entry describes choroid plexus cysts and the importance of genetic counseling. See **https://en.wikipedia.org/wiki/Choroid_plexus_cyst**.

Decompression of left atrium:

- Catheterization and Cardiovascular Interventions Journal. This academic article looks at the use of extracorporeal membrane oxygenation. See **http://www.ncbi.nlm.nih.gov/pubmed/10348539**.

- Critical Care Medicine. "Decompression of the Left Atrium during Extracorporeal Membrane Oxygenation Using a Transseptal Cannula Incorporated into the Circuit." This dense academic article explores the use of extracorporeal membrane oxygenation. See **http://www.ncbi.nlm.nih.gov/pubmed/16915115**. (Too dense to be really useful.)

- Interactive Cardiovascular and Thoracic Surgery Journal. "Blade and Balloon Atrial Septostomy for Left Heart Decompression in Patients with Severe Ventricular Dysfunction on Extracorporeal Membrane Oxygenation." This academic article looks at the challenges associated with use of extracorporeal membrane oxygenation. See **http://icvts.oxfordjournals.org/content/10/5/672.full**.

- Korean Circulation Journal. "Percutaneous Transseptal Left Atrial Drainage for Decompression of the Left Heart in an Adult Patient during Percutaneous Cardiopulmonary Support." This English-language academic article presents a case study of a patient with hemophagocytic lymphohistiocytosis, as presented with left ventricular dysfunction and cardiac arrest. See **http://www.ncbi.nlm.nih.gov/pmc/articles/PMC3152736 /**.

Echocardiograms:

- Group Health Cooperative. This webpage outlines the various types of echocardiograms, their processes and purposes. See **https://www.ghc.org/kbase/topic.jhtml?docId=hw21269 2.**

- Mayo Clinic. This site outlines the process of an echocardiogram, including preparation, risks, and what you can expect during the process.

See **http://www.mayoclinic.org/tests-procedures/echocardiogram/basics/definition/PRC-20013918.**

- WebMD. This webpage describes the various types of echocardiograms and their purposes, required preparation, and risks. See **http://www.webmd.com/heart-disease/echocardiogram.**

Emotional support for parents:

- Birth Defect Research for Children. This website and nonprofit organization provides information about birth defects and support services for children and parents. See **http://www.birthdefects.org/.**

- HealthTalk. This website provides access to other parents of children with congenital heart disease as well as resources and information. See **http://www.healthtalk.org/peoples-experiences/heart-disease/parents-children-congenital-heart-disease/sources-support.**

- KidsHealth. This site offers content on support for parents of kids who are sick or have special needs, as well as information on managing home health, marriage advice, and thoughts on caring for the siblings involved. See **http://kidshealth.org/en/parents/parents-support.html**.

- KidNeeds. This site provides professional opinions, links to programs and services, and connection with other families in similar situations. See **http://www.kidneeds.com/.**

- Kids with Heart National Association for Children's Heart Disorders. Started as a local support group, this organization offers support, education, and awareness through local events and an online listserv. See **http://kidswithheart.org/page/about-us**.

- Little Hearts, Inc. A national organization that offers support, education, resources, and networking opportunities to families dealing with congenital heart defects. See **https://www.littlehearts.org/**.

- Mended Little Hearts. This nonprofit organization provides hope and support to the "littlest heart patients of all," with more than eighty chapters in the United States and Mexico. See **http://www.mendedlittlehearts.org/about.shtml.**

- National Institutes of Health. This scientific paper, "Insights from Parents about Caring for a Child with Birth Defects," published in the International Journal of Environmental Research and Public Health, addresses the way having a child with a birth defects affects the whole family. See **http://www.ncbi.nlm.nih.gov/pmc/articles/PMC3774449 /.**

Epinephrine:

- Wikipedia. This encyclopedia entry describes epinephrine, its medical uses, adverse effects, physiological effects, pathology, mechanism of action, and role in culture. See **https://en.wikipedia.org/wiki/Epinephrine**.

General heart info:

- National Cancer Institute. This website provides an overview of the heart structure and functioning, including layers, chambers, valves, and blood pathways. See **http://training.seer.cancer.gov/anatomy/cardiovascular/ heart/structure.html**.

Heart block:

- Cleveland Clinic. This brief webpage describes heart block and talks about risk factors and causes. See **http://my.clevelandclinic.org/services/heart/disorders/ar rhythmia/heart-block**.

- Heart Rhythm Society. This website discusses a slow heart beat (or heart block), its definition, types, symptoms, and risk factors. See **http://www.hrsonline.org/Patient-Resources/Heart-Diseases-Disorders/Heart-Block.**

- National Heart, Lung, and Blood Institute. Part of the National Institutes of Health, this organization offers a website that describes heart block and outlines patients' outlook. See **http://www.nhlbi.nih.gov/health/health-topics/topics/hb**.

Hybrid heart procedures:

- American Heart Association. This PDF focuses on pediatric therapeutic cardiac catheterization, detailing the various forms of sedation and the techniques involved. See **http://www.heart.org/idc/groups/heart-public/@wcm/@hcm/documents/downloadable/ucm_30 7680.pdf.**

- Nationwide Children's Hospital. This website provides a parents' resource guide to HLHS. See **http://www.nationwidechildrens.org/hypoplastic-left-heart-syndrome.**

- Seattle Children's Hospital. This webpage briefly describes hybrid heart procedures. See **http://www.seattlechildrens.org/clinics-programs/heart/treatments-and-services/hybrid-heart-procedures/.**

- Seminars in Thoracic and Cardiovascular Surgery Journal. "Hybrid Procedures in Pediatric Cardiac Surgery." This academic article describes the emerging indications and techniques in hybrid pediatric cardiac surgery. See **http://www.ncbi.nlm.nih.gov/pubmed/15818362**.

- University of Chicago Medical Center. This article, dated 2004, outlines the historic significance of the hybrid approach to treating HLHS. See **http://www.uchospitals.edu/news/2004/20041018-hybrid.html.**

Hypoplastic left heart syndrome (general):

- American Academy of Pediatrics Congenital Heart Public Health Consortium. This nonprofit was organized to provide information and support for families affected by congenital heart disease. See See **https://www.aap.org/en-us/advocacy-and-policy/aap-health-initiatives/chphc/Pages/default.aspx**

- American Heart Association. Organized in a Q and A format, this website discusses the condition, its causes, and treatments, outlining the various surgical procedures involved in treatment. See **https://www.heart.org/idc/groups/heart-public/@wcm/@hcm/documents/downloadable/ucm_307664.pdf**.

- Children's Hospital of Philadelphia. This page contains a description and information on signs and symptoms, testing and diagnosis, treatment, and follow-up care with many clear illustrations. See **http://www.chop.edu/conditions-diseases/hypoplastic-left-heart-syndrome-hlhs/about#.Vm-IfF6RQpt**.

- Cincinnati Children's Hospital Medical Center. This webpage focuses on the Norwood Procedure, a surgical treatment for HLHS. See **http://www.cincinnatichildrens.org/health/h/hlhs/**.

- CongenitalHeartDefects.com. This site provides information to members of the worldwide congenital heart defect community. See **http://www.congenitalheartdefects.com/**.

- Centers for Disease Control and Prevention. Here, there is information about the condition's frequency, causes and risk factors, diagnosis, and treatment. See **http://www.cdc.gov/ncbddd/heartdefects/hlhs.html**.

- Fetal Health Foundation. Still under construction, this site will provide information on the condition as well as assist in finding hospitals that specialize in treating the syndrome. See **http://www.fetalhealthfoundation.org/**.

- Genetic and Rare Diseases Information Center. Created by two agencies of the National Institutes of Health, this center provides timely access to experienced information specialists who can answer questions in both English and Spanish. See **https://rarediseases.info.nih.gov/gard.**

- Heart Institute Encyclopedia. Provides easily accessible information about cardiac diseases, defects, disorders, and problems that may affect a child's heart. See **https://www.cincinnatichildrens.org/patients/child/ency clopedia/**.

- Mayo Clinic. This site provides an overview of the condition and discusses symptoms and causes, diagnosis and treatment, and management of the condition. See **http://www.mayoclinic.org/diseases-conditions/hypoplastic-left-heart-syndrome/home/ovc-20164178**.

- Medline Plus of the U.S. National Library of Medicine. On this website, you can learn about the causes, symptoms, exams, and tests, treatment, prognosis, and possible complications. See **https://www.nlm.nih.gov/medlineplus/ency/article/00110 6.htm**.

- National Heart, Lung, and Blood Institute. This website offers medical information about a variety of congenital heart defects. See **http://www.nhlbi.nih.gov/health/health-topics/topics/chd**.

- National Organization for Rare Disorders. Here you find a general discussion of the condition as well as information on signs and symptoms, causes, affected populations, standard and investigational therapies, and related disorders.

See **http://rarediseases.org/rare-diseases/hypoplastic-left-heart-syndrome/**.

- WebMD. Provides a basic overview of the condition. See **http://www.webmd.com/heart-disease/hypoplastic-left-heart-syndrome.**

- Wikipedia. This webpage describes the signs and symptoms, causes, management, prognosis, and epidemiology of the condition. See **https://en.wikipedia.org/wiki/Hypoplastic_left_heart_sy ndrome**.

Metabolic acidosis:

- MedLine Plus. This website discusses metabolic acidosis, including its definition, symptoms, diagnosis, treatment, and prognosis. See **https://www.nlm.nih.gov/medlineplus/ency/article/00033 5.htm.**

- WebMD. This clear definition of metabolic acidosis discusses causes, symptoms, testing, treatment, and prevention. See **http://www.webmd.com/a-to-z-guides/what-is-metabolic-acidosis.**

- Wikipedia. For an encyclopedia entry, this item on metabolic acidosis is fairly complex. See **https://en.wikipedia.org/wiki/Metabolic_acidosis**.

Oxygen saturation:

- American Association of Critical-Care Nurses. This section of the association's procedural manual describes the process of performing this noninvasive monitoring technique. See **http://www.aacn.org/wd/practice/docs/ch_14_po.pdf.**

- Nonin Medical, Inc. This webpage from a manufacturer of noninvasive medical monitoring devices outlines the purpose and process of using a pulse oximeter. See **http://www.nonin.com/Normal-Oxygen-Level**.

- Wikipedia. This encyclopedia article defines and outlines the process of oxygen saturation. See **https://en.wikipedia.org/wiki/Oxygen_saturation_%28 medicine%29.**

Patent ductus arteriosus:

- American Heart Association. This webpage sketches the condition and provides links for further information on how it affects pediatric and adult patients. See **http://www.heart.org/HEARTORG/Conditions/Congeni talHeartDefects/AboutCongenitalHeartDefects/Patent-Ductus-Arteriosus-PDA_UCM_307032_Article.jsp#.**

- Mayo Clinic. With several web pages devoted to the condition, this site includes symptoms, causes, risk factors, complications, diagnosis, treatment, and lifestyle and home remedies. See **http://www.mayoclinic.org/diseases-conditions/patent-ductus-arteriosus/basics/definition/con-20028530.**

- MedicineNet.com. This brief webpage provides a description of the condition. See **http://www.medicinenet.com/script/main/art.asp?articla rti=4798.**

- MedlinePlus. This webpage discusses patent ductus arteriosus, its causes, symptoms, diagnosis, treatment, and outlook. See **https://www.nlm.nih.gov/medlineplus/ency/article/00156 0.htm.**

- Wikipedia. This encyclopedia entry discusses the signs and symptoms of the condition, its causes, diagnosis, prevention, treatment, and prognosis. See **https://en.wikipedia.org/wiki/Patent_ductus_arteriosus.**

Percutaneous balloon atrial septostomy:

- American Heart Journal. "Percutaneous Balloon Atrial Septostomy in Infants with Transposition of the Great Arteries." This academic article discusses percutaneous balloon septostomy atrial in infants. See **http://www.ncbi.nlm.nih.gov/pubmed/1266719**.

- Arteriosclerosis, Thrombosis, and Vascular Biology Journal. "Balloon Atrial Septostomy: History and Technique." This academic article summarizes the mechanisms of prostaglandin generation. See **http://www.ncbi.nlm.nih.gov/pmc/articles/PMC3232558 /.**

- The Hospital for Sick Children. This brief webpage describes the process of balloon atrial septostomy. See **http://www.aboutkidshealth.ca/en/resourcecentres/cong enitalheartconditions/treatmentofcongenitalheartconditi ons/heartcatheterization/pages/balloon-atrial-septostomy.aspx.**

- Wikipedia. This encyclopedia page focuses on the surgical procedure on the top two heart chambers, outlining the indications and procedure. See **https://en.wikipedia.org/wiki/Atrial_septostomy**.

Prostaglandins:

- Journal of Arteriosclerosis, Thrombosis, and Vascular Biology. "Prostaglandins and Inflammation." This highly academic article outlines the mechanisms of prostaglandin generation and its role in modulating the inflammatory response. See **http://www.ncbi.nlm.nih.gov/pmc/articles/PMC3081099 /.** (Not terribly useful.)

- University of Iowa Children's Hospital. This webpage delineates the use of prostaglandin E for heart defects. It details the indication, administration, and response and

duration of action. See
http://www.uichildrens.org/childrens-content.aspx?id=234424.

- Wikipedia. This encyclopedia entry discusses the physiologically active lipid compounds, their biochemistry, function, types, and role in pharmacology. See **https://en.wikipedia.org/wiki/Prostaglandin**.

- WebMD. This webpage provides an overview of congenital heart defects. See **http://www.webmd.com/heart-disease/tc/congenital-heart-defects-prostaglandins-and-prostaglandin-inhibitors-topic-overview.**

Pulmonary venous congestion:

- The Free Dictionary. This item provides a dictionary definition of pulmonary congestion. See **http://medical-dictionary.thefreedictionary.com/pulmonary+congestion.** (Actually about pulmonary congestion, but useful.)

- HealthTap. This item provides a brief overview of pulmonary congestion. See **https://www.healthtap.com/topics/congestion**.

- Revista Espanola de Cardiologia. "Pulmonary Congestion in Acute Heart Failure: From Hemodynamics to Lung Injury and Barrier Dysfunction." This English-language academic article reviews pulmonary congestion in acute heart failure. See **http://www.revespcardiol.org/en/pulmonary-congestion-in-acute-heart/articulo/90025492/.** (Actually about pulmonary congestion.)

Septal defects:

- Centers for Disease Control and Prevention. This site provides facts about ventricular septal defect. See **http://www.cdc.gov/ncbddd/heartdefects/VentricularSeptalDefect.html.**

- Medline Plus. This website looks at atrial septal defect, its causes, diagnosis, treatment, outlook, and prevention. See **https://www.nlm.nih.gov/medlineplus/ency/article/00015 7.htm**.

- WebMD. This website provides an overview of ventricular septal defect, outlining causes, symptoms, testing, treatment (medical and surgical), and follow-up. See **http://www.webmd.com/heart-disease/ventricular- septal-defect?print=true**.

Sinusoids:

- American Heart Association. This webpage looks at single ventricle defects, including HLHS. See **http://www.heart.org/HEARTORG/Conditions/Congeni talHeartDefects/AboutCongenitalHeartDefects/Single- Ventricle-Defects_UCM_307037_Article.jsp#**.

- Circulation (journal). "Hypoplastic Left Heart Syndrome with Left Ventricular Myocardial Sinusoids: Echocardiographic and Angiographic Findings in the First Neonate Surviving the Norwood I and II Procedure." This academic article is a technical case study of an infant with HLHS. See **http://circ.ahajournals.org/content/117/17/e319.full**.

- The Free Dictionary. This dictionary entry defines sinusoid. See **http://medical- dictionary.thefreedictionary.com/sinusoid**.

- Journal of the American College of Cardiology. "Right Ventricular Infarction with Cardiac Rupture in an Infant with Pulmonary Valve Atresia with Intact Ventricular Septum." This academic article from 1983 is a case study of an eight-day-old infant with HLHS. See **http://www.sciencedirect.com/science/article/pii/S07351 09783801764**.

- Revista Española de Cardiologia. "Pulmonary Atresia with

Intact Ventricular Septum Associated with Severe Aortic Stenosis." This English-language academic article considers pulmonary atresia, which is a complete obstruction of the right ventricular outflow tract. See **http://www.revespcardiol.org/en/pulmonary-atresia-with-intact-ventricular/articulo/13055369/.**

- UpToDate. This website discusses congenital and pediatric coronary artery abnormalities. See **http://www.uptodate.com/contents/congenital-and-pediatric-coronary-artery-abnormalities.**

- Wikipedia. This brief encyclopedia entry defines sinusoid. See **https://en.wikipedia.org/wiki/Sinusoid_%28blood_vessel%29.** (Not at all helpful.)

Sinus tachycardia:

- American Journal of Cardiology. "Heart Rate Variability in Inappropriate Sinus Tachycardia." This journal article outlines heart rate variability in patients with inappropriate sinus tachycardia. See **http://www.ncbi.nlm.nih.gov/pubmed/9723649.**

- European Heart Journal. "Heart Rate Variability and Inappropriate Sinus Tachycardia after Catheter Ablation of Supraventricular Tachycardia." This academic article discusses the link between sinus tachycardia and radiofrequency catheter ablation of supraventricular tachycardia. See **http://www.ncbi.nlm.nih.gov/pubmed/8881859.**

- European Heart Journal. "Heart Rate Variability and Inappropriate Sinus Tachycardia after Catheter Ablation of Supraventricular Tachycardia." This academic article discusses the link between sinus tachycardia and radiofrequency catheter ablation of supraventricular tachycardia. See **http://eurheartj.oxfordjournals.org/content/16/11/1637.**

- Journal of the American College of Cardiology. This clearly written academic article outlines inappropriate sinus tachycardia syndrome. "Inappropriate Sinus Tachycardia." See **http://content.onlinejacc.org/article.aspx?articleid=1486 711.**

- MedicineNet.com. This webpage defines sinus tachycardia. See **http://www.medicinenet.com/script/main/art.asp?article key=9743.**

- UpToDate. This item discusses evaluation and management of the condition. See **http://www.uptodate.com/contents/sinus-tachycardia-evaluation-and-management.**

- Wikipedia. This encyclopedia entry discusses sinus tachycardia, touching on signs and symptoms, causes, diagnosis, and treatment of the condition. See **https://en.wikipedia.org/wiki/Sinus_tachycardia.**

Three-stage surgery:

- University of California–San Francisco Medical Center. This webpage describes the three-stage surgical procedure, called staged palliation or heart transplant, for HLHS. See **http://pediatricct.surgery.ucsf.edu/conditions--procedures/fontan-operation.aspx.**

Transvenous pacer wire:

- Medscape. This webpage details the process of conducting transvenous cardiac pacing technique. See **http://emedicine.medscape.com/article/80659-technique.**

- University of Ottawa Heart Institute. See **http://www.ottawaheart.ca/content_documents/Pacing_presentation.pdf.**

- Wikipedia. This encyclopedia entry features transvenous cardiac pacing, also called endocardial pacing, which is an intervention used to correct profound bradycardia. See **https://en.wikipedia.org/wiki/Transvenous_pacing**.

Two-vessel umbilical cord:

- Wikipedia. This site describes the condition when there is only one umbilical artery in the umbilical cord. See **https://en.wikipedia.org/wiki/Single_umbilical_artery**.

Wolf-Hirschhorn syndrome:

- Genetics Home Reference. This website, maintained by the National Institutes of Health, describes the condition and explains the genetic issues as well as the processes of diagnosis and management. See **http://ghr.nlm.nih.gov/condition/wolf-hirschhorn-syndrome**.

- WebMD. This webpage provides a brief description of the rare chromosomal disorder. See **http://www.webmd.com/children/wolf-hirschhorn-syndrome.**

- Wikipedia. This encyclopedia entry describes the condition, its signs and symptoms, epidemiology, and the genetics involved. See **https://en.wikipedia.org/wiki/Wolf%E2%80%93Hirschhorn_syndrome.**

- Wolfhirschhorn.org. This nonprofit organization's website describes the condition as well as its diagnosis, treatment and management, and prognosis. It also contains several family stories. **http://wolfhirschhorn.org/about-wolf-hirschhorn-syndrome/.**

Wound VAC therapy:

- U.S. Food and Drug Administration. This reprint of an

article from Nursing 2010 ("Negative Pressure Wound Therapy: Use with Care") outlines the potential challenges associated with the use of negative pressure wound therapy. See **http://www.fda.gov/MedicalDevices/Safety/AlertsandNotices/TipsandArticlesonDeviceSafety/ucm225038.htm.**

- Wikipedia. This encyclopedia article provides an overview of negative-pressure wound therapy. See **https://en.wikipedia.org/wiki/Negative-pressure_wound_therapy**.

- World Wide Wounds. This webpage discusses the process of vacuum-assisted wound closure, also called vacuum therapy, vacuum sealing, or topical negative pressure therapy. See **http://www.worldwidewounds.com/2001/may/Thomas/Vacuum-Assisted-Closure.html.**

www.ingramcontent.com/pod-product-compliance
Lightning Source LLC
Chambersburg PA
CBHW071453070426
42452CB00039B/1174